FINDING HOPE

*A Field Guide for Families
Affected by Addiction*

 LANCE LANG
WITH DR. WENDELL AND PAM LANG

Published by:

the
treehouse
group, llc

P.O. Box 1301, Harrisburg, NC 28075
thgroup.net

ISBN: 978-0-9903118-1-2
Printed in the United States of America
Library of Congress Cataloging-in-Publication Data

All scripture quotations, unless otherwise indicated are taken from The Holy Bible, English Standard Version® (ESV®) Copyright © 2001 by Crossway, a publishing ministry of Good News Publishers. All rights reserved. ESV Text Edition: 2007.

For information regarding author interviews or speaking engagements, please contact the public relations department – Lance@LanceLang.com.

1

WHY THIS? WHY NOW?

I was deep into my addiction the first time my dad asked me an important question.

I was probably easily taking 40-50 pills a day, cashing out IRAs left and right, stealing cash any chance I could get, and rummaging through my girlfriend's jewelry, hoping to find something that might bring $20 or $30 at the pawn shop. (I'd later find out she'd already shipped all the real stuff back to her parents because she knew I'd eventually start looking).

I was in real bad shape when he asked me, "Son, have you ever thought about going to AA?"

I looked up at him sharply, dozens of excuses running through my mind.

Which one should I use? I thought. *I'll need to keep at least two or three excuses in reserve in case he asks me again in a few weeks.*

I had no idea what AA was, why I should go, or what addiction was all about. And honestly, I don't think my dad did either.

I quickly circled back around to the thought of just telling him I would go, and then bailing once I left the house.

And that's just what I ended up doing.

I didn't *totally* mean to.

I wound up searching Google for some AA meetings in the area, found one with a convenient time, and took off toward it with plans to attend. But those plans only lasted a few fleeting moments. At the last minute, that evil voice in my head told me I didn't really have a problem, and that lots of people snorted prescription pain medicine that wasn't theirs (even while at work!).

And I believed the voice in my head.

Instead of a meeting, I ended up in the electronics department at Wal-Mart, watching the same jaguar run in slow motion across an African plain for 45 minutes. I loaded back into my car, drove home, and of course, about a half-hour later, my phone rang.

"How did it go?" my dad asked.

"Uh… great," I said, trying to expand my lie with some details that might make sense, but that I could easily remember.

I quickly settled on, "Yeah, uh, they were really nice and told me to come back next week."

He bought it, and that was that.

The first real encounter with recovery or sobriety my dad and I really ever had was now in the books. We both did what we naturally knew to do: he suggested something he thought might help and I lied.

Neither of us knew anything about the issue we were facing, but this story is a great example of what most parents or spouses try to do for their loved ones—and what most addicts do in response.

Unfortunately, if we're going to see ourselves in this story, we must also see that this line of thinking simply doesn't work. No one I know has found recovery because of a casual suggestion, and no parent can help their child when the relationship's baseline is dishonesty.

Tempted to give up? Throw in the towel? Throw up your hands in frustration? That's okay. That's natural. But don't stop there, because there's hope!

Sure, you might be asking yourself right now:

How do I help my loved one get help?

What can I do to help mend the brokenness in my family?

What should I tell them?

Who should we call?

What do we DO? We need HELP!

I promise you this: we will get there! But first things first. We have to talk about the WHYs before we can move on to the WHATs.

Why a Book for Families?

Have you ever watched the television show *Scandal*?

I'll be honest, I love that show. I know it's not for everybody, but when I found out about it, I couldn't help but love it—even to the point of once watching 50 episodes in less than a week (Yeah, I'm an addict for sure; once I start watching a show, I just can't stop! No doubt, Netflix can be my enemy).

Anyway the show is about a dynamic woman named Olivia Pope, who works as a crisis manager specializing in political situations, making her a perfect fit for the show's Washington, DC setting.

But on the show, no one calls her a *crisis manager;* Olivia is really known as a *fixer.* When major political or legal crises happen, Olivia gets called in to fix the situation. And let me tell you—she's good at it. She covers all the bases, never misses an angle, and there is rarely a problem she can't fix (minus the whole dramatic presidential affair that seems to be a never-ending plot line).

When Olivia Pope sees a problem, her first instinct is to fix it.

Many parents, spouses, and family members of addicts *think exactly the same way*. They see a problem and they want to fix it! They want to call in Olivia Pope! Or worse yet: they think they *are* Olivia Pope!

Many family members—parents, especially—truly believe that if the person they love has a problem, then they've got the solution.

But the problem is, Olivia Pope is not real. She's based on a real person, yes, but ultimately, she's a written character on a TV show whom always comes out on top in the end.

You are not Olivia Pope. You cannot fix every situation, and it's this crazy analogy that has led me to write this book (finally, all my binge-watching is paying off for the good of others!).

So that's the bad news: you're not Olivia Pope.

But let me tell you some good news: you are naturally programmed to think of yourself as Olivia Pope. For you moms and dads out there, you've been playing the fixer role since your little one was born. If there was a diaper blowout, you fixed it. If there was a problem at school, you fixed it. When dinner needed to be made, you fixed it. For your child's entire existence, you've probably been there to fix them.

I get it, really I do. I've had two children myself. Neither of them are ~~yet~~ teenagers at the time of this writing, but I can recall many times already that I've gone into fixer mode.

One night specifically comes to mind.

My son Ben was about five and somehow made his way into my bed in the middle of one night, arranging himself between me and the night stand. He was right on the edge when I suddenly felt him slide off the bed. Before I knew it, he hit the ground with a loud crash and started screaming. Loudly.

My mind immediately woke up and recalled the glass of water I'd left on that nightstand. Over the next few milliseconds, I thought, *Oh no, he's cut his head open or a shard of glass has pierced his body. He'll never look the same again, he's going to be disfigured, and he'll never be invited to prom! Oh my what am I going to do?* It's crazy how quickly our minds can jump to the worst possible outcomes—like not going to prom.

Anyway back to the story: I sprang into action, flipping on the light switch, scooping Ben up, and rushing him to the bathroom.

There was blood. It was everywhere.

I freaked out. Scoured his body for the wound. I found it on his right leg, where I also found a huge gash and chunk of muscle staring back at me. I instantly went into *MacGyver* mode: I ripped off my shirt, tore it in half, and tied a tourniquet around the wound.

Two minutes later, we were in my truck and headed to the hospital.

It's these types of moments that train our brain to think that when someone we love is hurting or wounded, we have the power to heal them, help them, or make it all go away.

It's not easy to accept the reality that this is nowhere near the truth.

Spouses, you know what I am talking about, as well. How many times have you thought you could change the person you married? Maybe you thought you could change them once you said, "I do," and only found out after the fact that it doesn't really work that way.

Sorry about that.

Anyone who's been married or in a serious adult relationship knows the struggle is real when it comes to trying to change your partner. Coming to realize that we cannot fix another human being is tough. But it's necessary.

For the past few years, God has changed my scenery somewhat. Not my physical surroundings—I still live and work with recovering men as I have for several years—but my *emotional* surroundings have changed.

My deep desires, the passions that keep me up at night, the thoughts that consume my rarely settled mind… God has been tugging on my heart for not only the men or women struggling or in early sobriety, but their parents and spouses. My heart hurts for them.

For you.

I've heard your stories of heartache;

I've listened as you've begged and pleaded with me to help your spouses.

I've witnessed you grieve the loss of your children.

I've observed you from afar, watching this vicious disease seep from your son or daughter to your entire family. Slowly impacting every relationship and skewing the dynamic completely.

I've watched siblings dismiss themselves from families altogether. I've watched couples get divorced.

I've watch as addiction destroyed your family and left you hopeless.

It's too much.

It's from this impression that God has made on my heart, that I have chosen to write this book.

I'm not the kind of person who sits on the sidelines and watches as people suffer. I can't stand it and I won't allow myself to selfishly hold on to what I believe God has called me to give away. The hope I've been given wasn't given to *just* set me free—it was gifted to be given away.

Now, I don't claim to have the perfect solution to knit

every family back together, but I do believe I have some experience, some resources, and some hope to give that can help you navigate the painful path of addiction.

You can't fix this problem, but that doesn't mean all is lost. You may not be Olivia Pope, but you *can* be living in hope.

Why You and Your Parents?

You may be wondering, since I was the addict and not the family member *affected by* the addict, whether I even have the platform to talk about this stuff. And I would agree that your question is a good one.

But my parents have been affected by an addict. Me.

They lived through this; they learned what to do (and what not to do); and they experienced firsthand the emotional devastation and turmoil that addicts can cause those they love.

It's one of the highlights of my life to have my mom and dad collaborating with me on this book. We all have a great deal of experience working with families, though my dad's experience far outweighs mine.

My father, Wendell, has been a pastor for over thirty years and has spent *months* of his life sitting on couches and behind desks listening to families talk about the struggles piercing their homes.

But it's not his experiences in the counseling office or behind the pulpit that will prove valuable to you in this book. What makes this collection of pages so special is our diverse and distinct relationships with addiction. His from the parent's standpoint, watching as I obliterated my life, and trying all kinds of ways to help me. And my opposite outlook.

It's this counterbalance of our voices that makes for an interesting blend that I think will give you a newfound perspective on addiction.

As a family, we've lived through this and come out (mostly) healthy on the other side. Every painful moment you may be experiencing today, every stabbing heartache you undergo as you watch your loved one stay actively addicted, we've gone through. We've experienced that level of pain—from both sides—and we've made it. We've endured the same struggle, so we know how it feels.

I've manipulated, conned, and lied to my parents for years. I made them cry, I hurt their hearts, and I refused to get help.

I wrecked every relationship in my life and left my parents in the rubble, trying to rebuild on my behalf. Problem was, they didn't have all the pieces, nor did they have any idea what they were supposed to construct.

I devastated my own life and blamed it on them. I went silent for weeks. I stole from them. I embarrassed them.

I simply did all the things us addicts do.

But we found some hope, and as a family, walked through the early days of recovery together.

When it was time to get help, my parents were there. When I detoxed and begged them to take me home, they were there. When I needed them to stand strong and resilient, they were there. When it was time for treatment, my parents drove me. As I began to move forward in my life of sobriety and needed some help getting back on my feet, they were there.

Whatever we've done, we've done it together.

When I found recovery, so did my parents.

Overall we've been through some crazy stuff over the past ten years or so.

The road of recovery can be a rocky one, which is why you need a steady hand to hold. If you don't have that, you have a lot less of a chance to make it.

For me, that steady hand belonged to my mother and father. And that's why we wrote this together.

Why We Wrote This

The most common comment I hear from the loved one of an addict is this:

"We just don't know what to do."

Now this is really a tough thing to hear. Imagine a family at their wits' end, pouring out their heart and soul to you, witnessing the sheer devastation that hangs over every word they utter, and then they make that statement. They say it, hoping against hope that it won't just bounce off you; hoping that maybe *you* have something to give them to make this all go away.

It's a daunting place to find yourself.

Parents, spouses, siblings, and all of those who find themselves in this position, professing that painful statement... you are exactly why we wrote this book.

The fact is: loved ones of addicts are lost.

They're clueless about how to deal with the epidemic of addiction that is attacking our world. They have been shamed into thinking that what's going on inside their four walls is not happening anywhere else in the world , which leaves them feeling alone, hopeless, depressed, and angry.

These emotions begin to settle into their family's foundation, cracking it, and tilting it in destructive directions. They turn away from their faith, lose the love inside their marriage, and sometimes forget who they are.

Time after time, addiction wins. Families are devastated, parents get divorced, and children get lost in the shuffle.

It isn't fair, it isn't right, and it shouldn't be this way.

I spend most of my workday with parents, listening to their stories, guiding them to the most helpful resources, working with their children, and counseling them the best way I can. Over the past few years, I've worked with over 200 families, specifically surrounding the topic of addiction. On top of that, in early 2015, Hope is Alive Ministries (the nonprofit organization I founded) started a support group for loved ones of addicts, called Finding Hope. It was this class that really began to open my eyes to the pain families were experiencing and the hope that could be found through the power of a community and the restorative nature of our God.

Why Should I Keep Reading?

Let me be clear from the get-go. This book will not outline ten steps to get your kid to stop smoking meth or seven ways to make your husband drink less and be nicer.

There is no such process. As I tell our Finding Hope support group classes, helping people find sobriety does not come with an easy button. This is not a Staples commercial.

I wish it was. I wish I could give you a step-by-step guide, but I can't. *No such thing exists, because everyone's process out of addiction is different.*

But what I can do is to tell you the truth. I can tell you real-life stories of how people have found solutions to these devastating problems. I can pass along advice from educated people who work in this profession, and counsel people like you every day.

So that's what you'll find in these pages.

Ultimately, we want this book to be the key that helps you navigate the map of your family's situation.

No family is the same, nor is their plight. But we have found that inside each story of addiction, pain, or life-altering situation, there are similar solutions that can be applied to help people find hope. There are programs, communities, common practices, and, most importantly, other people who have walked down the very same road you're on.

Our goal is to pass along the Hope we have found, so that you too might come to experience the great joy and freedom that comes when you find what you've been looking for.

We pray this book shows you that recovery for the addict and the family is possible.

We pray that this book reminds you that you are not alone.

We pray that this book helps you step out from under the shame.

We pray that this book speaks to you in your specific situation.

We pray that this book gives you much needed clarity.

We pray that this book helps you find hope.

2

WE'RE ALL A LITTLE CRAZY

I don't have any statistics on this, but I would venture to say that one of the more common adjectives used to describe people that we don't understand is: "crazy."

Think about it. How many times have you said…

"He's crazy."

"She's crazy."

"They're crazy."

"Her husband is crazy."

"That chick is straight-up crazy."

"He's got a little crazy in him."

"Wow, that family is crazy."

Let me just get this out in the clear early on. *We're* all *a little crazy.* So the next time you call someone crazy, just realize that you are right there with them.

Now, I *will* admit there are varying degrees of crazy. There's the Charles Manson crazy, the Dennis Rodman crazy, and the Evel Knievel crazy. There's the Steve O crazy, there's the mother-in-law-in-the-movies crazy, and then there's all the *other* kinds of crazy in between.

The enemy longs to see you shamed into a corner, and he has a special tool just for you and your family. It's this devastating tool he uses, leaving you stuck in your home, lonely, tired, depressed, and angry at whatever has happened to you. It's this tool that he uses to keep you and your family from being the beacon of hope that you can really be. It's what he wants to wedge in between you and the rest of your loved ones. It's how he is planning to break up your marriage.

I bet you think I'm going to say that tool is *addiction*, but it isn't.

This tool the enemy uses to destroy families is *pride*.

I don't mean pride as you traditionally may view it, in the sense that you are arrogant or conceited. Rather, I'm talking about the type of pride that convinces you that what you are dealing with is an isolated incident, and no one else is struggling with something similar.

The pride that says a wayward child, a drug-addicted spouse, or an alcoholic mother is something that shouldn't be mentioned in polite conversation. I mean the kind of pride that lies to us and holds us back.

This pride makes us feel like we have to have it all together. This pride keeps us from opening up about the reality of what's really going on in our lives. It barricades us from the rest of the world, and makes us think we are crazy.

But remember: *we're* all *a little crazy.*

My experience has shown me that the world is addicted to acting like our lives are fine and dandy, and we will go to great lengths to display this. Lying, manipulating, buying things we don't need, and the like, and all to make everyone else think everything in our family is okay.

Nothing to see here, gang! Look at the smiling photo I just posted on Facebook! We're great!

Let's get real. Everything in your family is not okay. And *that's* okay!

In fact, that should be refreshing. You should feel lighter as you read this. Your family is jacked-up, and so is mine, and so is everyone else's. We are all broken people living in broken world. We shouldn't be surprised when addiction, despair, and pain hit our lives—we should be prepared for *when* those things hit eventually.

I work with people from all types of backgrounds, colors, denominations, and income levels, and the one common thread throughout them all is this: every family thinks everyone else is okay, while they're the crazy ones.

I think God, in his infinite wisdom, has an interesting way of helping us broaden our scope of pain and expanding our understanding of others brokenness. Or more simply put, God uses our hurt to help us understand others' hurt.

Now, maybe that raises some theological eyebrows in the room, so let me tell you what I mean by that.

For most of my early twenties, I was a judgmental jerk who thought he was better than everyone else and who looked down on certain types of people. Specifically: people who were addicted, depressed, and unemployed. I didn't understand people like this and honestly thought of them as pretty weak. I thought of people with addiction issues as junkies and losers who were pathetic and had no use in the world. And don't get me started on depression. I mean seriously? What is so hard about just being happy?

During that time in my life, someone very close to me was suffering through depression. It made me livid to watch her mope around, never wanting to do anything, always tired, and generally not having any passion.

But the people who *really* made me mad were those who were unemployed. This was just not acceptable to me. I would watch grown men get laid off, and from my vantage point, they just sat around and waited for the next job to come to them, never getting out and pursuing one themselves. I thought that if that were ever me, I would humble myself the very next day and go to MacDonald's and get a job flipping hamburgers for minimum wage to support my family.

What is wrong with these people, I would think. *They're all just crazy!*

I had judgment down pat. Heck, I was an *expert* at it.

Well, fast-forward five years and guess what three experiences God allowed me to experience? Yep, you nailed it! Drug addiction, depression, and unemployment.

I became the "weak" drug addict who just couldn't quit and looked pathetic. I fell into countless bouts of depression and began to realize just how incredibly difficult it is to even breathe when real depression stuns your soul. And on top of that, I got laid off, found myself filling out unemployment papers, and lying on the couch, overwhelmed with stress and nearly paralyzed with fear about what I was going to do with the rest of my life.

You see, what I thought was crazy, God began to use to help me realize it was very real. What I thought would never happen to me, happened. What I thought was a problem for "those" people, became a problem for me.

Crazy hit home and changed my entire perspective.

I know many of you can relate to this. You had the idyllic version of life in front of you, and somewhere along the journey, it changed. What you thought was going to be a picturesque landscape, now looked like a Picasso. But let me remind you, a "mediocre" Picasso painting recently sold at auction for

$173 million.

Your crazy isn't crazy; it has intrinsic value. Why? Because there is splendor even in the chaos. There is something beautiful in the brokenness. God does his best work when things don't look perfect.

He's perfect so we don't have to be.

He came for the sick, not the healthy.

We can have hope knowing that our lives are crazy—and that's exactly where God wants us. When we are weak, we can finally begin to look to the one who is strong!

This is foundational to understanding all that will come in the rest of this book. There is not a fully sane person among us, so it's time to stop pretending there are.

Sure, there will still be people in your world who don't want to acknowledge their crazy, but you don't have to let that affect you—you can still acknowledge yours.

We are all broken people. Brokenness is ubiquitous. It's everywhere we are, everywhere we go. We can't escape it.

Your crazy doesn't make you a bad person, a failed partner, or a disastrous parent. What it makes you is real, honest, and human. This flawed world is where flawed people live. So accept the craziness that is in your life.

I cannot emphasize enough how critical that understanding is for where we are going. Fully accepting the situation you find yourself in today will help you walk through the battle that lies before you tomorrow, and beyond.

Don't let pride keep you from claiming your pain. It's the most freeing thing you can do.

(After each chapter my parents will chime in with their perspective on the previous chapter, here's the first take.)

Parents Perspective: Wendell Lang

From a parents' point of view, we all want to view our families as functional and healthy. However, in the spirit of transparency, we are all surrounded by dysfunctional people, thus we all have dysfunctional families.

Pride is the forerunner of all sins. Pride is self-absorbed. Pride can reveal either how miserable we are or how wonderful we are. In Isaiah 14:13-14, we even see that pride is what made Lucifer the devil.

Until we are able distance ourselves from our children's choices, we will continue to be weighed down by the subtlety of sinful pride. We are so prone to take credit for our children's *good* choices, that we feel embarrassed when our children make *poor* choices.

Bottom line: our responsibility as parents is to "train up" our children. We simply cannot make choices for our children as they grow into adulthood.

I remember wondering what our community would think of me as a local pastor when it became evident that my son was making poor life choices and had become a drug addict. Perhaps you have read the well circulated poem about pride, "Pride is a Great Cheater":

My name is Pride, I am a cheater. I cheat you of your God-given destiny... because you demand your own way.

I cheat you of contentment...because "you deserve better than this."

I cheat you of knowledge because you already know it all.

I cheat you of healing because you are too full of me to forgive.

I cheat you of holiness because you refuse to admit when you are wrong.

I cheat you of vision because you would rather look at a mirror than out a window.

I cheat you of genuine friendship because nobody is going to know the real you.

I cheat you of love because real romance demands sacrifice.

I cheat you of greatness in heaven because you are not going to wash anybody's feet on earth.

I cheat you of God's glory because I convince you to

seek your own.

My name is pride, I'm a cheater. You like me because you think I'm always looking for you. Untrue.

I'm looking to make a fool of you.

God has so much for you, I admit, but don't worry…If you stick with me you will never know.

Only when we crucify our personal pride and shame over our children's actions, will we be able to come alongside our children and become a part of the solution.

When we disembark the pride ride, we can start the healing process that each parent desires and deserves. We must love our children enough to eradicate our egos for the sake of healing from the albatross of addiction.

I love the old hymn writer Isaac Watts who penned, "When I survey The Wondrous Cross"

When I survey the wondrous cross

On which the Prince of Glory died

My richest gain I count but loss

And pour contempt on all my pride

3

HOUSTON, I THINK WE HAVE A PROBLEM

Most people have heard the notion that the first step to dealing with a problem is admitting it. But this is only part of the equation, and if you haven't spent any time inside the rooms of Alcoholics Anonymous or Al-Anon, you likely haven't really heard the entire first step. It says this:

We admitted we were powerless over alcohol—that our lives had become unmanageable.

It's that second part, the *unmanageable* part that I think most people miss.

It's also the hardest part for a parent to decipher.

What makes an addict an "addict"? At what point do they cross the line? What does an unmanageable life look like?

What percentage of their income do they need to start spending on their drug of choice before we call it a problem? Does it only become an addiction if they tip over into doing illegal things? What about smoking weed, is that okay because it's legal in some states? Is there just some way to *know for sure* when my loved one's life has become unmanageable?

These are all great questions; hopefully you'll have some answers to by the end of this chapter.

But there's no *single* answer to any of them. Every person's situation is different; every addict's story has its own plot twists and roster of characters. And because of this, I thought it might be easier if I just listed the top ten signs that you have a problem in your situation.

Now, you may see one or two of these, but that doesn't necessarily mean your child, spouse, parent, or distant relative needs immediate intervention. You'll have to use some of your own discretion to discern that (we'll tackle that later in the book). But these are good indicators that something is going on under the surface that needs attention.

Once we begin to see a problem come to light, it means it's probably been festering in the dark for some time.

Think of a plant: long before you begin to see the fruit, you know there's a lot going on underground: roots are forming and spreading, and more energy is pushing up out of the ground, from the dark to the light.

So let's take a look at some common indicators that

something awful has taken root in your love one's life.

Signs You've Got A Problem On Your Hands

1) Dishonesty

Drug addicts have a tough time being honest. "Tough time" is playing nice, actually—drug addicts find honesty practically impossible.

My Dad commonly says that dishonesty is the number one trait of an addict, and I agree with him. We will lie about anything and everything. We'll lie about our past, we'll lie about our jobs, we'll lie about our health, we'll lie about where we've been, we'll lie about where we're going—we'll lie about the weather if we think we can get away with it (or even if we don't).

There are really no limits to our hypocrisy. We will lie about whatever, whenever, however if it serves our purpose.

Lying in general (and lying for no reason specifically) is a huge sign that something is not right.

But you probably already know this or you wouldn't be reading this book. Addicts are horrible manipulators, and we will let our dishonesty run rampant while we're in active addiction.

It's hard to really believe anything an addict says. So if you are early on in this journey and you are beginning to see dishonesty rear its ugly head, then be warned: it's probably only going to get worse.

But at least now you know what you are dealing with.

2) *You Find Something*

I've heard all kinds of stories on this topic. Parents and spouses finding bottles in the shower, weed under the mattress, pills swapped out and hidden in unsuspecting containers, and of course my old go to, hiding powders in my Carmex container.

Regardless of how creative your loved one can get, once you find something, it should be sign that problems are on the horizon. And furthermore when you find something on their person, in their car, in a pocket, stuffed in a drawer or anywhere else, it's theirs. Don't let them ever tell you otherwise.

We are the best finger pointers in the game, and it's always easier to make our parents or loved ones believe that someone else is the problem and we just so happen to be in the wrong place at the wrong time.

Finding drugs, alcohol or paraphernalia of any type is a clear sign that you've got a problem.

3) *MIA*

Another telltale sign that something is up, is when your

loved one goes MIA.

This seems to be fairly obvious, but you'd be surprised at the number of people who tell me, "Well, we haven't seen him in a few weeks."

"Have you called him!?" I ask. "Gone by his house, driven by his work?"

"No, we were just trying to give him space."

C'mon, people! When you are in the stages of trying to decipher what is going on in the life of your loved one, not seeing them or hearing from them in weeks is a giant, blinking, warning light indicating that you need to do something. Especially when they start missing family functions or routine events that used to mean something to them (birthday celebrations, watching the football game on Saturdays, fishing with Dad, or any other activity that would seem out of character for them to miss out on).

Continued absence = problem.

4) Something doesn't smell right

If they walk in your house reeking of weed, then you've probably got an issue.

If you don't know what weed smells like, but they smell funny, then it's probably weed. The same goes for cigarette smoke, which is often used to mask other drug smells.

Other drugs can bring smells as well. Making meth produces powerful odors that may smell like ammonia or ether. These odors have been compared to the smell of cat urine or rotten eggs.

If they suddenly smell like something other than themselves, then that could be a sign they're up to no good.

5) Something doesn't look right

Smell is just one sense that can tip you off that something needs to be addressed. Sight is another.

Even if you're looking at the world through a pair of thick coke-bottle lenses, your eyes are great tools to utilize when trying to understand what is going on with your loved one. What do they *look* like? What does their physical appearance tell you?

Are their eyes bloodshot? That could be a sign of marijuana use.

Or you can determine other potential drugs by looking at the pupils. Some drugs, like alcohol and opioids, cause the pupils to constrict. Others, like amphetamine, cocaine, LSD, and mescaline cause them to dilate.

Police officers know this; some use it as one way of checking if someone is off their face. They generally look for pupils dilated either to less than 3mm or more than 6.5 mm.

Other visual signs:

Teeth Clenched

Nodding off and walking up repeatedly

Frequent use of the bathroom

Limited sleeping

Always wearing long sleeves (to cover track marks from needles)

Unexplained weight loss or gain

6) Change in Influences

Looking back on my journey, I think one of my main early indicators could have been the change in my friend scene.

Toward the end of my time in high school, I practically swapped out friend groups in a matter of months. I went from the Normal Party Crew to the Excessive Party Crew. And on top of that, I practically moved in with this new group. I spent just about every waking moment with them, which meant I was getting high just about every waking moment.

This change in influences was a critical part of my path to drug addiction.

If you're seeing similar behavior in your loved one, it might be time to wake up to what's really going on.

7) *Isolation*

Just as switching out friends was a great sign that I was changing inside, so was my sudden tendency towards isolation.

This doesn't mean that plain old introverts are closet or potential addicts—some people just need to get away by themselves frequently—but as my addiction really began to settle in, I became more and more reclusive and isolated. I didn't want anyone at my house and I just really didn't want to be around people in general. I would make excuses to leave events early, or even better, simply never show up in the first place. If I did happen to get to work, I would shut and lock the door to my office, opening only for certain people.

The worse I got, the more isolated I became.

8) *Money, Money, Money, Moooooney…..Money!*

Yeah, this is a big one.

As drug use begins, or addiction sets in, the money requests skyrocket. And remember sign #1: addicts will lie, lie, lie to your face, and they will *especially* lie about why they need money.

Fundraising requests can come in a variety of dishonest ways; addicts will trade on their health, on their kids, on their kids' health—I've done them all. I could go through hundreds of different types of specific scenarios, but I think you get the gist: when money requests begin to increase at the same time other suspect behavior increases, then something is probably not right.

9) Stealing

If we can't get it by asking, we'll get it by taking.

We will steal just about anything. It becomes a sick and twisted form of thinking that tells us: *If it's going to bring monetary value to me, then I have the right to take it.*

In the midst of my addiction, I started jacking everything. Money from wallets, Dad's golf clubs, Mom's earrings, Sister's pill bottles, Grandma's hair looms, girlfriends' purses, our employers' printers, food from the gas station, TVs from Wal-Mart... if it wasn't bolted down, and I was left alone with it, it probably came with me so I could sell it or pawn it to get my next fix.

If your stuff goes suddenly missing, your loved one might be in trouble.

10) Emotional Swings

Drugs and alcohol have the unique ability to shut down our emotions, turning addicts into cold, callous, manipulative, self-serving monsters. And then, in the rare cases when we allow the buzz to wear off, we can become over-the-top, dramatic, tear-filled, remorseful, and *almost* kind.

Should you see us in one of these non-buzzed states, feel free to enjoy it, but *don't for a minute think we're all better.* In fact, it's these types of swings that you as the loved one need to be looking out for.

If you're loved one is shut-off part of the week, and then bawling like a baby over the weekend, you might have a problem on your hands. Especially, if one of more of the other factors is simultaneously at play.

While this is not an exhaustive list, it does cover the broader, more far-reaching signs that you need to be aware of. But while being aware of those signs is one thing, being willing to do something about them is something else entirely.

Why?

I'm going to speak mainly to moms and dads right here: as parents, we all want to believe the best about our kids. When they tell us something, we want to believe it's true, and sometimes we will go to great lengths, and contort our thoughts into jaw-dropping positions in order to believe what they tell us. Even if we're not very coordinated, we can perform Olympic-level mental gymnastics to convince ourselves that our kids are fine, trustworthy, and honest.

It reminds me of a time in high school when my dad found a bag of marijuana in my Jeep. He sat me down in our living room and confronted me with that age-old question that's been handed down from anti-drug PSAs and that so many people like me have been asked: "Is this yours?"

Stop right there. See, while this may feel right to you as a parent, it's actually the wrong way to start altogether. I was doing terribly in school, but I was a Ph.D. candidate in lying and manipulation.

With that one question, he set me up to lie to him. I'm blaming it all on him! Ha! It's *his* fault, right? I wish it was that easy, but we know it's not.

Anyway, my dad didn't mean to open up the dishonesty gate with that question, but he did, and I went through it faster than Aragorn riding into Helm's Deep.

So, here's a quick tip: if you find something in your loved one's car, room, locker, jacket, jeans pockets, stuffed under their mattress, or on their computer, then just know this: *it's theirs.* Don't let them tell you otherwise.

It's always theirs.

Of course that bag of weed was mine! A much better way for my father to start the conversation would have probably been, "Lance, we know this is yours, so what are we going to do about it?"

But anyway, back to the story. There we were in the living room, and Dad asked the question.

"No!" I lied. "I don't even know what that is." I exaggeratedly scrutinized it. "What is it?"

My dad told me that he thought it was marijuana, and I played dumb at first, then made up some story on the spot about how someone must not like me and that they must've put that marijuana under the floorboard of my Jeep to try to get me in trouble!

Well, not only did my dad believe me—because parents tend to *want* to believe that their kids aren't doing drugs, but instead are being set up by some other kids—but he wanted to verify that it was really a bag of weed and make sure it got disposed of properly.

So he called the police.

And a member of the Fraternal Order of Police of Pryor, Oklahoma was soon at my doorstep. And then he was in our living room, sitting across from me and my dad, staring a hole through me, *knowing* that it's mine. But he couldn't do anything about it because I wouldn't admit to it, and my dad had totally bought my story.

I was sweating bullets! But not so much that I couldn't maintain my lie enough to convince my dad (and therefore the police officer) that I was innocent. It was terrifying, but eventually the cop left (but not without taking my weed with him!) and my dad and I were left in silence. My heart was racing, but the conversation soon ended and I let out a huge exhale that I'd gotten out of that jam.

And then I went out that night and got high.

Houston: I had a problem.

We want to believe the best about our kids. That's what

makes us great as parents! But we also have to learn to admit that. Oftentimes, the problem is right in front us.

We just don't want to see it.

(Throughout the book, I've inserted interviews I've done with men that live in HIA's Mentoring Homes and other recovering addicts I know. The interviews are specifically directed towards the previous chapter's subject matter. Here's the first set of interview.)

Interviews with other addicts: The Anonymous Athlete

Would you like the world to know your name?

No.

Who were you before you really became addicted?

I was a great student. An exuberant, outgoing person who always wanted to be surrounded by people, and people wanted to be around me. I loved to have fun and never wanted to sit still. I was a standout athlete with big dreams. I had a work ethic that was second to none, and I was as dependable as any teenager out there, maybe even more so. I took care of myself physically, and was proud of who I was.

When did you start using?

I used all kinds of things recreationally all throughout my teenage years, beginning with marijuana and alcohol at about [age] 12 or 13, and progressed to "party drugs," things heavier in immediate effect and consequence, as I worked my way through junior high and high school.

When did you know you had a problem?

I think I began to realize I had a problem when I was about 24. By this time I had already begun my career, gotten married and purchased a home with my wife.

My career carries a lot of inherent stress, and at my young age, I had no idea how to handle that stress, but I knew I could make it temporarily cease as long as I was using.

I began to use as often as I could get my hands on something. I think at this point, I knew there was a problem, but I also "knew" I could control it myself with a little discipline.

I was wrong!

What were some of the things you lied about?

I primarily lied to my parents about where I was, and when I was there.

My dad was very well connected in our small town, so I got caught in those lies often. The bigger problem was that my dad is also an alcoholic/addict, and I knew how to manipulate him to avoid punishment.

He made some very poor decisions during my childhood that negatively affected me and my family, and being the manipulative "future addict" that I was, I was able to play that to my favor.

I knew he felt bad for the things he had done, and because of that I knew I could get away with *anything* because he felt as though he had to make up for my difficult childhood by being soft on me.

What specifically did you do to hide your drug use from your parents or spouse?

I went to great lengths to hide my use from my wife. For the better part of two or three years, she was oblivious to my use, as she had never been around it at any other point in her life.

When she started to get wise to it, I would work long, long hours so I could use at work… by the time I'd get home from work, she'd already be in bed and I didn't have to worry about covering any tracks.

When I was home, I would wait for her to go to bed, [then] use once she was down, having used enough during the day to get me through those few hours until she was out.

I also used anger and temper tantrums to either run her out of the house, or get her to want me to leave, and then I'd go use.

I was literally destroying my marriage and my sweet wife's amazing spirit, to feed my addiction. And last, if all else failed, I would lie, lie, lie, lie, lie. There was no lie I wouldn't tell. I didn't care how hurtful or destructive it may end up being.

I had to get my fix.

When did your loved ones realize there was serious problem?

I don't know that my parents ever realized it. I don't know if they have realized it to this very day, and I've been through multiple stints in treatment and live in a recovery environment with several other men. My parents were my absolute greatest enablers. They assisted me [during] eight to ten years of destructive addiction. Sometimes wittingly, other times not.

My dad became my primary drug dealer all the way up to my first day of sobriety.

I recently had to make an incredibly difficult decision and cut off contact with my parents. I love them dearly, and it wasn't easy to do, but I know I've made the right decision. My prayer is that someday they'll recognize the enabling and the co-dependency that exists in their lives, and that they can over-come it, at which point we can begin to rebuild our relation-ship. Until then, that relationship will remain the most danger-ous threat to my sobriety, and I have to treat it as such.

(A couple times in the book, I've inserted interviews I've done with professionals that I work with and whose work I recommend. The interviews are specifically directed towards the previous chapter's subject matter. Here's the first profes-sional interview.)

Interview with a Counselor: Sheila Ridley, M.Ed., LCSW

[Note: Sheila Ridley is a Licensed Clinical Social Worker for the Second Story Ranch Recovery Community, and is certified by the Oklahoma Department of Mental Health and Substance Abuse for Residential Co-Occurring (Substance abuse and mental health) and Extended Care Provider. Find out more about them by visiting SecondStoryRanch.com, or by calling 405-679-0023. Ms. Ridley graciously agreed to provide some counselor-informed context to this chapter.]

In your experience what are the early signs that some-one is struggling with an addiction?

The most obvious sign of addiction is a change in behavior, or what might appear as a change in personality. These signs may include lying, stealing, lack of motivation, secrecy, new friends, an unexplainable increased need for money, and mood swings including irritability and paranoia.

Oftentimes, in addition to the behavior change, a physical change is observable as well, including decreased hygiene, acne, blood-shot eyes, decreased appetite often resulting in noticeable weight loss and dilated pupils.

What's a common problem you see in the parents of those addicts who check into your facility?

Oftentimes, parents are seeking a diagnosis that can be identified and treated with a pill.

"Just tell me what is wrong with him/her so he/she can get better."

Addiction can be a tough pill to swallow, pardon the pun, for many parents as they feel a responsibility for their child's addiction. A mental health diagnosis is most often seen as no one's fault and includes a recipe for "getting better, including a prescription"… in short, an "easy fix".

I see all too frequently, parents and spouses wanting recovery more than the addict, and working at it harder than the addict. Over-responsibility of the loved ones is a common challenge.

If the addict is not sincerely more interested in his or

her own recovery, they likely will not create sustainable recovery. If you are working harder than the addict, *STOP*.

Loved ones also seem to have a difficult time trusting the process. I recently had a father, who was a dentist, attempt to tell me what his son needed. We came to an agreement that I would not come to his office and fill teeth and he would not tell me how to treat his son for addiction. In the kindest voice I could muster, I told him if he knew how to help his son, he would not need me or Second Story Ranch as he would have already done it himself.

What are some common traits of addicts?

Addicts are some of the brightest, most charming members of the human race. They are usually smart as a whip, magnetic, entertaining… and full of crap. They lie to everyone and themselves so often, they [eventually] believe the lies they are telling.

On the flip side, they usually have very low self-esteem, oftentimes to the point of self-hate. They can be underachievers, finding meaning in very little. Spirituality is non-existent, and many believe there is no God, often taking on radical beliefs that are very different from the beliefs they have been taught.

One of the families I worked with that were of strong Christian faith, were baffled that their son claimed to be atheist and was against democracy. They could not understand his thought process, asking me and themselves, "Where did we go wrong?"

How can a parent begin to confront issues like dishonesty, theft, and anger?

One word: *boundaries.*

Do not start tolerating behavior that you have never tolerated before, and know that you should never tolerate. Don't make excuses for the addict or yourself. *Always*, even when you want to wring their necks, speak to the addict with love and respect. Be intentional in the choice of your words and tone of voice.

Think about speaking to the addict in a way to bring them closer to you, not push them away. Develop agreements, (notice the word *agreements*, not *rules*) and establish consequences for not adhering to the agreements. Enforce the consequences *every single time*! Don't set the consequences if you are not ready to enforce them. There's nothing worse than a parent or spouse looking like a wet dishrag because they won't keep their end of the agreement.

If you can't keep your end of the agreement, you certainly can't expect the addict to keep theirs.

If a parent were to call you today and tell you they think their son or daughter is abusing drugs, what would you tell them to do?

Find out for sure: get a drug test. Contact a therapist specializing in addiction that can help you navigate the conversation with the addict about the results. If you ask the suspected addict to take a drug test and they're resistant, then put on your helmet, as the road ahead could be uncharted.

Go to Al-Anon and/or a support group. As a mother, Al-Anon kept me out of an orange jump suit ...not a good color for me!

There is no such thing as too much support. Make no excuses like lack of time or not liking Al-Anon. The sooner you face the situation head on, the sooner you get to take the helmet off.

What is the best thing a parent can do to help their addicted child?

Pray for him/her and yourself. One of the things I pray for (as the mother of a 26-year-old addict who has been in and out of recovery since the age of 14) is to ask for words and wisdom so my son could hear.

In short, pray and get out of the way. Always remember, God loves the addict more than you do.

Be consistent in the love and care of your child... love them too much to participate in the behaviors of addiction.

Set boundaries. The addict must have an enabler to stay active in addiction… don't be that person.

Go to Al-Anon. Get help, help, and more help… and support. You are not crazy, although you may feel that way. You will need words outside of yourself, your spouse/family, and the addict to hear and know the truth. Addiction really distorts reality!

Parents' Perspective: Wendell Lang

The medical and recovery communities may have many symptoms for and byproducts from addictions, but for families and parents, there is no greater evidence of addiction than lying.

"Liar, liar, pants on fire" should be the official motto of the addict. Addicts will lie with a straight face. They will lie about nonsensical issues. They will even lie when it would be easier to tell the truth.

Romans 7:18 reads, "I know that nothing good lives in me, that is, in my sinful nature. For I have the desire to do what is good, but I cannot carry it out." When we lie, we play God. We deny our humanity and try to control everything for selfish reasons. The addict is often in a state denial—and that's not a River in Egypt. God says in Jeremiah 17:9, "The heart is deceitful above all things and beyond cure."

Like most addicts, Lance was a professional-grade liar.

As a parent, I have often wondered if I knew he was lying and ignored it, or if I simply wanted to believe the best in my child. Addictive children bring their parents and families into addictive and enabling behavior patterns. We can become liars and deniers in our own lives, to the point where we lie to ourselves!

Far too often, a parent will sweep a child's addiction under the rug.

My experience was that, as parents, we simply didn't know what to do, so we dove into the river of denial.

Today there are many recovery programs that will prove helpful when your family falls prey to addiction.

You'll never go any further toward recovery or refreshment until you admit you are helpless. Helplessness embraces the truth.

Here are a few confessions to help you do just that:

I can't change my past. But God wants me to forget those things which are behind and press on toward the goal He has for me. He is a God who says, "See, I am doing a new thing!" (Isaiah 43:19)

I can't control other people. We have a tendency to want to fix others. Remember…"I can do all things through Christ who strengthens me." (Philippians 4:13)

I can't cope with my pain…alone. We need each other. Go to a group meeting. See a counselor. Find an AA, NA, or Celebrate Recovery meeting. "And if a man prevail against him that is alone, two shall withstand him; and a threefold cord is not quickly broken." (Ecclesiastes 4:12)

We have all heard the misquotation, "God helps those who help themselves." That's *not* in the Bible. Actually, the opposite is true: God only helps those who admit they're helpless.

4

JUST ADMIT IT, IT'S EASIER

In the last chapter, we talked about all the different signs and indicators that something might be going on in your family. But there's a huge shift that takes *seeing* a problem, to the level of *admitting* the problem. And man, we do *not* like to admit problems, even when we see them.

As the saying goes: you're only as sick as your secrets.

This is especially rough for parents. In fact, I'd say the biggest problem I see in parents is when they refuse to even admit there's a problem within their family, even though that lack of admission directly prohibits their addicted loved one from admitting that they need help!

Some parents will do anything they possibly can to make sure no one thinks their family has issues. Well, we already established that everyone has issues, so you can't use that excuse anymore. We've begun to recognize what problems look like, so now it's time to own up to them and start admitting them.

Before we can do that, though, it might be helpful to understand why we don't want to admit to problems in the first place.

I think it's because it makes us uncomfortable to open up and get vulnerable.

If we admit to a problem, then we can think that's a potential weakness for someone to exploit, or it's a ding in our character, or it's a default that others will look down upon. It's the same reason we create these social media personalities, where we post only photos of us at our best, looking like we just have the best life of anyone on Facebook. Admitting a problem means exposing that façade as the lie that it is. And who wants to tear down something they've spent so much time constructing so carefully?

I also think there is a certain generational issue at play here, and I'm speaking primarily to parents when I say this. Most parents who are part of the Baby Boomer or early Generation X generations, grew up watching what their parents did. And those parents kept everything buttoned up tight. When things went wrong, they didn't tell the church, they didn't tell the community, and they certainly didn't try to find a counselor to talk about the issues they were facing.

No. Instead, the parents of a couple of generations ago just ignored their alcoholic brother or that sister who slept around. Those things weren't something you brought up in "polite company." And besides that, the church was viewed as an unsafe place to go in times of personal crisis. So they just kept everything to themselves.

The parents of our current generation grew up watching this, and when they became parents themselves, mimicked what they saw as kids. If something as huge as addiction sat down on the couch in their living room, they kept quiet about it, afraid of potential embarrassment or the judgmental attitudes of their neighbors or that one busybody at church.

Don't take this the wrong way, but *who cares*?

If people want to judge your family for having human beings in it, then those people have rendered their judgment unworthy of being noticed by you!

If they aren't going to be on your side with understanding and compassion, then they aren't worth impressing with a fake smile plastered across your face!

Choosing to tell someone about the issues you're dealing with? That's the real deal, and it's the first step you'll need to take toward finding hope.

Of course, admitting the problem is only the first mission to accomplish; after we admit our problems, we need to ask for help. But we can even find difficult!

Why?

I think that has a lot to do with the myth of self-reliance that our culture holds so dear. We'll admit that, yes, we have a problem, but we'll assume that it's *our* problem to handle, not anyone else's.

This is the kind of thinking that led my dad to suggest to me that I go to AA and then leave it at that (remember the story at the beginning of this book?). He was aware of the problem, even to the point of admitting it, but then he didn't seek out any outside help. He just did what he thought was best—which is admirable of him!

It's okay to admit that you aren't an expert on addiction and recovery. It's okay to seek out help. Trust me: you'll have enough work ahead to expend any extra energy trying to sustain some false narrative about the health of your family. Just admit it already.

But What Will Happen?

That's the big worry, the great unknown: you don't know what will happen when you *do* admit that your family is in trouble.

And when we don't know something, we can be afraid of it. So if you have a fear of admission, you're in great company!

But the crazy thing is—and I've seen this over and over—once you admit your problem, that very same problem gets easier to live with. It's much more work to keep your family's secret a secret. But the benefits of admitting your family's struggles far outweigh the hassles of tamping it down.

For one thing, when you admit your problem, you'll suddenly find people crawling out of the woodwork to say, "Me too!". It's crazy to find out how many of your coworkers, neighbors, friends, and fellow churchgoers have gone through the exact same thing.

Trust me: you're not alone in this.

Admission of your problem also provides a great opportunity to learn from those who've been through it.

Why bang your head against a wall when someone can come along and show you where the sledgehammer is?

You'll also find the willing arms of a community of people, a network of shoulders to cry on, hands to hold, and knees to hit in prayer. You don't have to endure your season of brokenness in isolation; admitting your problem will help you find a place to belong in the midst of your turmoil.

When you let people into your world, the more help, the more prayers, and the more accountability you'll have.

And who couldn't use more of that?

Parents' Perspective: Wendell Lang

The shame game is akin to the pride ride, but can manifest in many ways.

Do you ever stay up late when you know you need sleep? Do you ever take in more calories in a day than your body needs? Do you ever feel that you should exercise, but just don't? Do you ever look at some sexually explicit images on your computer you know are immoral, but you watch them anyway? Do you ever take prescription or illegal drugs you know you shouldn't, but you take them anyway? Have you known you should be unselfish, but you act selfishly instead? Have you ever tried to control someone or something and found them uncontrollable?

Before we can come to grips with dealing with our children's addictive propensities, we need to take a personal spiritual inventory. Once we have looked inward we can better deal with the social and cultural taboos of assisting our addictive children. Indeed, coming clean with the dirty, little family secrets is a huge step toward healing.

I admit that I have struggled with having an addictive child while believing I "practiced what I preached."

Teaching our children well is job one. But predispositions, innate temperaments, and family curses are also factors in our children's poor choices. I had to come to the realization that only through transparency and openness would our family ever have any hope of healing.

When we own our shortcomings as parents, and trust God with our kids, then we are able to lay the choices of our children squarely on *their* back. Then and only then can we admit that we have some family issues.

Of course we would all do some things differently as parents, but addiction is an illness, and hiding the illness serves no purpose. It would be paramount to feeling ashamed that our offspring has cancer.

There is a tendency to refuse to admit our struggle with hurts, hang-ups, and habits. The Bible helps us with admitting our pain. "You're blessed when you're saddened because it seems you've lost control. Only then can you be embraced by the One most dear to you." (Matthew 5:4, MSG) God has an antidote for denial—it's called pain. I agree with Rick Warren, who wrote, "We rarely change when we see the light, we change when we feel the heat. We don't change until our fear of change is exceeded by the pain."

We are prone to say, "I've got this thing," Sometimes God sends other people into our lives to help us see those blind spots. This is called an *intervention*! These are hard, painful experiences, but we must be willing to hurt someone's feelings in order to help them.

Even God has dealt with some of His children through interventions, like Isaiah, who said "Woe is me… I am a man of unclean lips," or Paul: "Oh wretched man am I, who shall deliver me form the body of death," or Peter: "Depart from me Lord for I am a sinful man." These are men who came to face to face with their faults and admitted them after God shone upon them.

Remember: the first step to healing is to admit that you have a problem.

5

IT'S NOT YOUR FAULT

I'd like to take a moment to talk about a famous scene in the film *Good Will Hunting* (no, not the one where Matt Damon slaps the phone number on the window of the bar and asks, "How you like them apples?"). It's a scene that takes place toward the end of the film (spoiler alert), after the troubled genius character of Will (played by Matt Damon) has spent a good bulk of the film's runtime reluctantly submitting to therapy sessions with Sean (played by Robin Williams, who won an Academy Award for his performance in the role).

Throughout the film, Will resents the time he has to spend with Sean, but as is the way in these types of stories, eventually the two form a sort of bond and each of them begins to see a breakthrough in their own stories.

The scene in question contains a riveting revelation: both Will and Sean were victims of child abuse. As the emotions pass over Will's eyes, Sean looks deeply into him and tells him, "It's not your fault."

And then he says it again. "It's not your fault."

And again. "It's not your fault."

Over and over and over, Sean tells Will the truth. Hammering it home through sheer repetition, each utterance another blow against Will's defenses and the self-defeating lies he's been telling himself.

Eventually, Sean has said it enough that Will begins to believe it, and he's left an honest, vulnerable man, aching tears billowing up and temporarily alleviating the pain he's kept down for so many years.

"It's not your fault" is a mind-blowingly liberating sentence, but it can be so incredibly hard to believe.

Nevertheless, that doesn't make it any less true for you today.

You might have a loved one who is an addict.

But you are not the one who made them that way.

What Happened

There are about as many reasons people get addicted to a mind-altering substance like drugs or alcohol, as there are people. No one's story is exactly the same, which is why I feel comfortable saying that there's not a person in the world who is immune to the disease of addiction.

Yes, some people are more prone to it (alcoholism has been shown to be hereditary), but everyone, given the "right" circumstances, could wind up veering into addictive territory. Addiction is like a virus or like The Borg in that old television show, *Star Trek: The Next Generation.*

Addiction doesn't care about anyone's family history or upbringing; it doesn't care about anyone's economic status or genetic makeup; it doesn't care about anyone's race, creed, or color. Addiction is no discriminator and will go after anyone and everyone.

That's why I can say it's not your fault.

There's a quote they use in Al-Anon, which is, to quote their literature, a "worldwide fellowship that offers a program of recovery for the families and friends of alcoholics," and it's a quote I love:

When it comes to addiction in your loved one, "you didn't *cause* it, you can't *control* it, and you can't *cure* it!"

Isn't that liberating? Read it again and let it sink in.

The person who is in active addiction is partially there because they are lying to themselves, and one of the big lies they'll tell to themselves is that their situation—when they even look around and have a glimmer of awareness that it's not a good one—is not their fault.

No. They want to believe that someone—anyone other than them—is to blame for the bad choices that have led them down this path.

Maybe they're trying to pin that blame on you. My advice: don't let them. They want to make you think you're at fault, and if you let that start to take root within your heart, the guilt can grow to debilitating degrees.

That's why you have to reject it.

They're the ones who are making the choices they make. Perhaps they made those choices out of a reaction to a terrible tragedy, or to a hurt or wound they sustained. While that's somewhat understandable, it does not make it excusable.

People are victims of tragedies every day; not everyone turns toward addiction to handle them.

That's why I can say with absolute certainty: it's not your fault.

As much as I would have liked to blame my parents for my problems, at the end of the day I was the one shoveling pills down my throat.

Did I struggle come to terms with the way they chose to handle a few situations? Yes, of course—what kid doesn't? But as I chose to accept them for who they were, I also began to accept my role in the play as well.

I was the chief problem, the main issue; I had something innately different about me, and until I dealt with that, I could never find sobriety.

Acceptance was and will always be the key to moving past all my problems.

Because it's not your fault. It was mine.

Parents' Perspective: Wendell Lang

I hope every parent of an addict will read and reread this chapter. Yes, over and over!

It is so easy for parents to take the pride ride or play the blame game, but there are multiple factors in addiction. The giant of guilt will attempt to slay you at every turn. The problem is that when we succumb to our Goliath-proportioned issues, we are rendered totally helpless in securing healing.

We have all taught our children about "guilt by association." As parents, we must be aware that we can often associate our sense of worth by our children's behavior. We have lived vicariously through our children. We tend to do this through sports, arts, and studies.

But when I was able to admit that my family was broken, it served as a reminder that I am a broken vessel. Celebrate Recovery groups remind their members that God cherishes broken things. In this world, we de-value broken things. In sports, if equipment is broken, you toss it. If a TV is broken, you may find it cheaper to get a newer (and bigger) one, so out it goes.

However, God values broken things:

The alabaster box of perfume had to be broken before the fragrance filled the room.

The five loaves and two fishes had to be broken before a miracle happened.

Jesus said, "This is my body which is *broken* for you."

Parents, addiction is not your fault, but it would be a shame to allow your pride or guilt or shame to remove you from getting involved in promoting healing and hope to your addictive child. None of us are pumped up about wearing the scarlet letter "A" (addict) around our neck, but may we always live out our overcoming as a badge of the grace of God in our lives!

6

THE FINE LINE: ENABLING VS. HELPING

When I was in high school, I had very little in the way of moral grounding, something I'm not proud of but which is key for understanding the way I acted in the story I'm about to tell you.

This story takes place during my senior year, when I was all the way gone into the party scene. I tried not to care one bit about the schooling part of school—I was only interested in what kinds of people school could put me in contact with that could help me party down.

It was during this time that I dated a lot, and as my senior year wound down, I found myself dating two different girls, possibly at the same time, and both of them older than me. They'd both gone to my high school and had the very same English teacher that I had: Mrs. Diems. But the similarities don't stop there: they'd also written their senior papers on the same topic: Charlemagne, the famous king of the early Middle Ages.

I knew I was going to have to write *my* senior paper eventually, and by now you can maybe guess where this story is headed. I managed to use my silver tongue to acquire the electronic versions of both my girlfriends' senior papers on Charlemagne and then literally copied and pasted different parts of them into one document, and turned it in as an attempt to pass off as my own.

I wasn't trying to impress Mrs. Deems so I could get an A (or even a B or a C); I just wanted to do enough so I could pass the class and graduate.

I handed that paper in with about a month left in the school year, and it wasn't long until my mom received a fairly irate phone call from Mrs. Deems, delivering the news that she was going to fail me in senior English—rendering me unable to graduate—unless I had a new paper to turn in. On the following Monday.

It was a Tuesday.

I had to turn around a brand new, fully cited, 20-30 page research paper, and I had less than a week to do it. And if I didn't do it, I wouldn't graduate.

I actually panicked. Not because I wanted the grade, but because I wanted to be done with school.

But you know who panicked even more? My dear mother.

She knew me, and what I was capable of at that time in my life. She knew that, if it were up to me and my efforts, that paper wouldn't even get *close* to done. She *also* wanted me to graduate on time, so she decided to help me.

By "help," I mean "write every word of my senior English paper for me."

Literally. Every word. I didn't even type in my name.

To this day, I have vivid memories of seeing her upstairs in the office of our home in Pryor, Oklahoma where I grew up, hard at work at the computer doing research and writing my paper for me.

I'll admit it: I felt *slightly* guilty about it at the time, but not enough to run up there and relieve her of the duty. If she wanted to help me, I was going to let her.

Besides, that meant I could go out and party with my friends.

She finished it, I turned it in, and guess what: I got a pretty decent grade on it! Good enough to walk across the stage at my graduation and get that diploma that my mom had earned for me.

God bless her, she was doing the best she knew to do at the time, and I don't fault her for it one bit.

But while she thought she was helping me, she was actually enabling me.

What Is Enabling?

You cross the line from helping to enabling when you start to shield your addicted loved one from the full consequences of their behavior. My Charlemagne story, while funny, is a perfect example of this.

I should not have graduated. I had slacked off the entire school year, and did not deserve the diploma I got. I was the one who turned in the original plagiarized paper, so I was the one who should've had to stay up late for a week, desperately working to create something that would get me a passing grade.

But that's not what happened. My mom—who is a lovely, lovely person who honestly thought she was doing the right thing—stepped in front of that no-graduate bullet and took it for me.

You can probably understand why. The reason we call these people "loved ones" is because we love them! We want to care for them and meet their needs, but the fact of the matter is: addicts are irrational, and in the throes of a disease that renders them uncaring. When you see them begin to stop caring for themselves, or for the world around them, you do the logical, human, empathetic thing and try to export *your* caring on to them.

The problem is: that doesn't work.

Instead, you wind up trying to control your loved one's behavior, which is always going to be a bad idea.

I know this sounds counterintuitive, because the things you want to do—assist, encourage, fix, protect, support, nurse, serve, accommodate—are all good things.

These are the kinds of things that good spouses do. They're the kinds of things that good parents do. They're the kinds of things that good family members do.

But when it comes to the addict, these good things become poison and the exact things that will keep everyone unhealthy.

When you enable, you prevent your addicted loved one from suffering any harmful consequences for their behavior—and if they don't suffer any consequences, they have no reason to change. Your help becomes something they can depend upon, therefore enabling them to continue living the lie that their disease is feeding them.

Do you see? Is this making sense to you? Are you feeling liberated yet? Is the unbearable weight of making yourself responsible for someone else's behavior lifting off your shoulders?

I hope so.

Enabling and Codependency: Fitting Together Like A Glove

Oftentimes, people will enable an addict because they're codependent on them. Codependency is a word that gets thrown around a lot in recovery circles, and some people are certain they're codependent when they aren't, while others are certain they aren't codependent when they actually would make a terrific textbook example.

So how can you know whether you're codependent? You can start by answering the following ten questions:

Do you seem to attract needy and dependent people and wonder why that always seems to happen to you?

Do you find it easier to be more concerned about other people than about yourself?

Do you find it difficult to hear and accept criticism, even when it's given lovingly?

Do you need or seek approval from those around you?

Do you feel guilty when you can't help someone that you feel responsible for, like you just aren't up to the task?

Would you rather give in to the will of others than defend yourself and stand up for what you believe in or demand what you want?

Would you stay in a difficult relationship or situation because you'd rather deal with the pain there than change?

Do you ever feel resentment for people when you help them?

Do you have an undefinable feeling that life is cheating you?

Do you have physical, stress-related symptoms like difficulty sleeping, stomach problems, tension in your back or neck, or headaches?

If you answered yes to most of those questions, you may be codependent. And if you're codependent, you're probably enabling.

So how can you know if your caring has turned to codependency?

Here are the eight most common characteristics of codependency; see if any of these sound like you.

Responsible

Codependent people feel responsible for others, but in a much more hyper, over-the-top way than your garden-variety responsibility. The codependent person takes so much responsibility that their own emotional wellbeing rises and falls on the behavior of the person they're trying to be responsible for.

Emotionally Confused

Codependent people have a very difficult time knowing how they feel. Ask them an emotion they might be feeling, and they likely will not be able even to identify it, let alone express it in a healthy way.

Afraid

Though they may not realize it at the surface level of their brain, codependent people are deeply afraid of being alone. This fear of abandonment leads them to dig in and stick with relationships that are hurting them, simply to avoid the isolation and pain that comes from being by themselves.

Perfectionistic

Codependent people tend to be perfectionists, holding up unrealistic expectations as a measurement tool for just about everything. But don't feel bad—they can be just as hard on themselves as they are on everyone else.

Repetitive

Those who are codependent will often find themselves repeating relationships with other dependent people, whether those people deal with alcohol or drug addiction, or to more socially acceptable addictions like food and work.

Reactive

Rather than acting on their own behalf—because that

might be too risky (and remember, they don't know how they feel)—codependent people are reactive. They react to situations, they react to other people, they react to just about anything, because being reactive makes more sense than being proactive.

Condescending

The codependent person can sometimes adequately be described as "a hot mess", because in the midst of their perfectionistic and reactive tendencies, they also often feel like a failure. But this is a deep sense of failure that works its way into their entire being, creating a low sense of self-worth and leading them to a great, yet unspoken, sense of condescension toward themselves.

Depressed

Lastly, the codependent person also often struggles with depression, and not the put-a-smile-on-it kind, but the long-lasting, medically diagnosable kind of depression that leads down many dark roads.

Now, just to be clear, you don't *have* to be codependent in order to enable your loved ones—I would say neither of my parents really fit into the codependency box, but they managed to enable me rather well (which is something they'll admit, right alongside the fact that they didn't know what they were doing, and were just trying to do the best that their uninformed selves could do).

Nevertheless, if these aspects of codependency ring true to you, then you might be enabling your loved one as well. That can be a very, very difficult truth to accept, and believe me—I understand if you're having difficulty with it. I know you love your son or daughter, your spouse, your parent, your family member—I know you want the best for them and want to help them in any way you can.

But I also know that enabling them is the opposite of help.

"The Best Thing My Mom Ever Did"

My good friend Floyd works down at Rob's Ranch, a treatment center in Central Oklahoma for men struggling with chemical dependency. He's the health and nutrition supervisor, and makes a point to spend time with many of the families each weekend as they arrive for visitation. In conversations around the dining room table, I've heard him tell parents this about hundred times...

"The best thing my mom ever did for me was leave me in jail."

It's always fun to see the responses, especially those who have loved ones caught up in the grips of addiction. If you're like that, you've probably wondered if you should have followed Floyd's mom's lead and done the same thing a time or two.

Leave them in jail

Leave them on the street

Don't give them any more money

Take away their car

Turn their phone off

Change your locks

What Ms. Carter did, saved her son's life. But it wasn't an easy decision. Allowing kids to reap the consequences of their choices never is.

But it's often the best thing you can do.

A few years ago, my then-eleven-year-old son asked me, with tears in his eyes, if he could quit football. He wasn't seeing any playing time, and some of the kids had been giving him a hard time.

"Please, Dad!" he pleaded, standing on that field after a just-finished practice, and staring me right in the eyes. "Let me quit!"

In that moment, I wanted to ease my son's pain, to let him off the hook, and give him a quick way to find relief. It seemed like the right decision; after all, he was hurting.

Letting him quit would've been the convenient decision. *But it was not the RIGHT decision.*

Yes, I could have let him walk off the field that night and instantly relieved the hurt and embarrassment he was feeling, but it would've only done so temporarily. Instead, all I would have done was bailed him out, set him up to be a quitter the rest of his life, or, worse yet, potentially crippled his ability to work through pain.

I'm so glad I didn't. Instead, I had a talk with him about pushing through difficult things, the power of perseverance, and all the ways he could grow if he just stuck with it for a little while longer.

He went back to practice the next day, and though not a lot changed for him in terms of the game of football, the character in his heart grew stronger, even if he didn't realize it.

Bailing our kids out is a natural reaction, and just to be clear: sometimes it makes sense. There are times when we do, as parents, need to rescue or advocate for our kids.

But I would say that, more often than not, we probably don't need to slap the training wheels back on our kids' lives.

It's tempting, though, because our brains and hearts justify that as love. We feel like the savior, the hero…. "Daddy or Mommy to the rescue!"

But what are we really saving them from?

Are we saving them from pain? Poisonous relationships? Prison time? Or are we just keeping them from learning vitally important life lessons—the types of lessons that will help them arrive at that crucial place where reality sets in, and help begins to make sense.

You see, each time we step in and take away the pleasure of earned consequences, we take one step closer to enabling, and they take one step closer to addiction.

The weight of enabling grows heavier and heavier as our kids turn to adults. And when you begin to enable your children, you begin to walk a fine line that typically doesn't end well.

I speak with families every week who look me in the eyes and say, "I know I've enabled him; I know we bailed him out one too many times." Each time I hear this, it scares me to my core.

Why?

Because this is a recipe for years of pain, guilt, and possibly an early death.

I get it—no one wants to watch their kids suffer. But if you are faced with a situation, as Ms. Carter was, when time and time again your child has made destructive choices while consistently looking to you to bail them out, I urge you to follow her lead.

Will that be easy? I've never had to go through it personally, but I can imagine it's one of the most difficult choices a parent might have to make. I know for a fact that Ms. Carter hated to see Floyd suffer, but look what happened: that suffering was temporary, and now on the other side of it there stands a man of character, endurance, and hope; a man who can testify that he *came through the suffering* and it turned out okay.

Sometimes the best thing a parent can do is to let go and let God do what he needs to do.

Interviews with other addicts: The Enabled Manipulator

How did your parents or spouse enable your further in your addiction?

My parents and girlfriend, whom I had spent the most time with and in communication with during my using, enabled me in several ways.

How did you use your parents enabling against them? How would you manipulate them?

With my parents, it was very easy to ask for financial help, because they rarely saw me in person and didn't know of my using after my first rehab. After turning down their offer of going to sober living after my first rehab, my parents basically set me out on my own. I went to live with my girlfriend's sister as a makeshift sober living house where the "rules" would be the same as any other sober living home. Her sister and husband had no clue what a sober living house was, so getting away with the old habits was far too easy.

My parents agreed to pay for my "rent" at the house, so all I needed to pay for was food. I quickly began to establish connections in the area to begin selling drugs again to be able to pay for my own supply of drugs. Because this was all done through cash transactions, my parents again had no idea what I was up to. Daily I would be in contact with my parents and sober living guardians to reassure them that I was fine and remaining sober.

As my "six months of sobriety" came closer, I began to lose control of my game of lies. My brain was not where it had been before, and I found myself struggling to get through each day.

I knew that my constant manipulation was going to backfire on me soon. I was tired of lying and not being able to remember which lie I had told to which person. Eventually, the inevitable caught up with me and I got caught in my lies. I lost a job I loved, relationships I cherished, and the trust of every person I had considered close to me.

If I could go back to the day I went into my first rehab for help, I would do things differently.

First of all, I would have listened to the people trying to help, instead of manipulating myself, and then others, into what I wanted.

For parents, enabling can come in many forms, but you cannot let your child or loved one do the things he or she says will help them. In most cases they are wrong, even if they think they are right.

Make them do the harder things instead of going easy on them, because the harder things will enable more growth. More accountability and communication will further the addict's sobriety, too.

I felt alone early on in my sobriety and wished I had more people considering my own feelings and ambitions. I wish I had been pushed harder to achieve the things I wanted instead of being let loose to figure out life on my own.

Interviews with other Addicts: The Parent-Playing CPA

How did your parents help further your addiction?

My parents felt guilty about their divorce and other things that had happened in my life, and out of that guilt they always gave me money or allowed me to take money I should not have been given, as well as making excuses for my behavior and not adhering to consequences.

How did you use your parents enabling against them? How would you manipulate them?

I would take anything I wanted by saying I needed it, or by acting like school was wearing on me and that I deserved it because I was working so hard at school and doing well.

How did your parents enabling prolong your addiction?

My parents enabling me allowed my addiction to go on for about 2 more years than it should have.

Did your parents ever try to put down boundaries? Were they successful?

Not really until towards the end. I went to Paris with my mom and brother, and I was on Xanax the entire trip; I was not easy to work with, and was very defiant. When we got back, my mom was very disappointed in me, but she never really cut me off from money or from allowing me to come to the house or anything like that.

What could your parents have done differently that might have helped your find sobriety sooner?

My parents should have cut me off from all money as soon as they realized how bad I was, and should not have bailed me out of jail, nor paid for my expensive lawyer when I got my second DUI.

I think part of the reason they didn't do anything about [my problem] was that I was still doing so well in school, and they wanted me to finish school more than they wanted me to go to rehab.

Looking back on it, I don't know if they made the right decision or not, because I do not know if I would have gone back to school after I went to rehab or not. On the other hand, if I had taken a break and gotten sober before I finished, I might have gotten a better job when I graduated, and been ready to take the CPA exam.

All I know is, things have worked out the way God wanted them to, and I am where I am today because my parents didn't give up on me. The last bit of money they spent on me was to send me to rehab, and when I went in they told me that this was the only rehab that they would pay for.

This time it worked.

A Word From A Counselor: Kyle McGraw

[Kyle McGraw is highly regarded as one of the premier drug and alcohol counselors in the state of Oklahoma. His background includes time spent as the Director of Substance Abuse Services for the Oklahoma Department of Human Services, the Executive Director of A Chance to Change Foundation, and Director of Counseling Services for Southern Nazarene University. In addition to that, he has and still maintains a thriving private practice in Edmond, Oklahoma, Transforming Life Counseling Center. For more information on Kyle, visit TLCCOK.com or call 405-761-1740.]

Why did you decide to dedicate your life to helping individuals and families overcome substance abuse problems?

I grew up in an alcoholic and abusive home. My parents did the best they could and the church youth group became a home away from home. I began working with youth full time after my college education and started helping, like many helped me in my teenage years.

My Senior Pastor challenged me to go to graduate school to further my abilities to work with youth.

My education has taught me that the family, not just the individual, has to change in order for the recovering individual to have a chance.

If an addict is ready and willing to get help, what is the plan of action that you normally give to them or to their family?

Often an immediate assessment to address whether or not the person needs medical detox is crucial. Addiction is a brain disease, and withdrawals often need medical supervision.

Secondly, I see what kind of "buy-in" there is among family members. Without family support, it will be more difficult for the addicted person to succeed. The disease of addiction is bigger than any one individual, and therefore takes many working together to achieve success.

Once the assessment takes place, and depending upon the severity of the disease, it's time to determine the level of care needed. That can mean outpatient, inpatient, or residential care.

In your opinion, does every drug addict need to go to treatment to find sobriety?

No! Sometimes this can be successful on an outpatient basis. The assessment of the individual and family, along with drug of choice, last usage, length of time, tolerance, and many other factors go into establishing a science-based assessment.

What's a common misconception about addiction that you hear from your patients?

One common misconception is thinking, "I can outsmart it by controlling it."

Secondly, is this myth, "I am gainfully employed, therefore I cannot be an addict."

Thirdly, is the myth, "I am married and have not had any serious consequences due to my usage." This is often known as "denial" to the addict.

Often a significant other or family member sees it differently and has a list of reasons why their loved one needs to quit and seek treatment. Often education with family and the affected individual needs to take place long before the addict ever wants help.

***What is the best advice you can give a mom or a dad
that is dealing with a child that is refusing to get help for
their addiction?***

Seek help for yourself even though your child refuses
help. When enabling stops—and often family members can be
in denial about their own enabling—then healing can begin.

Parents' Perspective: Wendell Lang

Psychologist and author M. Scott Peck has said, "Lazi-
ness is the single greatest impediment to spiritual growth." Let
me be clear from the outset: enabling rarely has a lazy bone
in its body. Rather, enabling often manifests itself in making
excuses and blaming others for your child's behavior. So often
parents truly believe they are helping but are really in the midst
of enablement.

When we enable our children we are traveling down
a slippery slope. When do we come alongside our child and
when do we exercise tough love? Every situation and circum-
stance are different, so outside perspective is often helpful—
seek counsel from those who are in recovery circles. It is amazing what an objective and experienced voice will lend during
your time of trial.

Far too often when we enable our children, we are simply fleshing out a guilt trip. When we own the decisions of our children, we feel it is necessary to make amends for their actions, and thus we enable our kids.

While some struggle with forgiving their children, other struggle with forgiving themselves. Fixing our family is more then we can do alone: we must replace our pain with God's peace.

"And the peace of God, which transcends all understanding, will guard your hearts and your minds in Christ Jesus." (Philippians 4:7) Mercy and forgiveness is God's supernatural way to deal with those who have hurt us. We are Christ like when we allow our loved ones to experience some pain in order to be healed. Groups like Celebrate Recovery, Al-Anon, and AA will help you find the fine line between helping and enabling so that you can stay on the right side of it.

7

SO NOW WHAT?

I hope you've come to the point of admitting that your loved one has a problem, that you may have unintentionally (or intentionally, who knows?) contributed to it by enabling them, and now you want them to find the help they need. You may even think that you can push them or coax them toward that help, maybe through your powers of persuasion or by intimidating them into it through some heavy-handed ultimatum.

Unfortunately, that's usually not the case. Most addicts will not respond to threats (they'll respond to the *consequences* of those, if they ever see them), and they will only listen to your well-intended, logical plea as long as they need to, in order to convince you to give them money.

No, most addicts, myself included, have to find their own reason to get help. You've probably heard it called "hitting rock bottom."

The Elusive Rock Bottom

I don't know how many times I've heard someone in the recovery community say, "Well they just haven't hit rock bottom yet." And every time I hear that, I always think to myself, *What does "rock bottom" look like anyway?*

Is it getting caught?

Is it prison time?

Homelessness?

Losing your family?

Do you have to be dirty, nasty, and smelly to *hit* rock bottom? Is there a place called *rock bottom* that people are actually hitting?

Well let me tell you, after working with hundreds of addicts the past few years I can confidently say… I have no idea what rock bottom is.

I really don't! **I have no clue.** I have found no way to identify whether someone has hit rock bottom or not. There is no glaring marker or checklist or brightly flashing indicator that can precisely qualify a person for rock-bottom status.

What I have found is this: rock bottom is different for everyone. And if that is the case, then why are we trying to guess when a person has or hasn't hit it?

I think we tend to have a somewhat romanticized view of what rock bottom looks like, based on the way movies, books, and television shows have portrayed spiraling descents into degradation. We expect rock-bottom to look something like getting busted by the cops, or turning tricks in the parking lot behind a grungy motel, or wasting away on a grimy couch in a trash-piled living room that is covered in pizza boxes, rat droppings, and a dingy haze.

But that's not at all how *my* rock bottom looked. Not for a second.

For the most part, I looked relatively normal at *my* rock bottom. **I had a good job,** I made great money, I went to church, I had a pretty girlfriend, I lived in a decent house, and I drove a nice car. Those are relatively material signs, but if you didn't know me, you would have no clue **I was simultaneously a** *full-fledged, 50-pill-a-day drug addict.* I was a fairly high-functioning addict who, from the world's point of view, was nowhere near rock bottom.

So how can you tell?

An addict's rock bottom can be about as camouflaged as a *Duck Dynasty* cast member on Saturday morning during duck season. They are impossible to find, and none look the same. So instead of using that as some type of crutch or justification to accept unacceptable behavior, you can use it as a catalyst to intervene early and often.

Because the truth is: we loved ones *can* force a rock bottom. It is possible. We can say "enough is enough". We can take away privileges, money, and freedom. We can force treatment, change the locks, and turn off the phone. We can fire someone, cut them out of the family business, ban them from our facility, or look at them right in the eyes and tell them that today is the day something changes.

You see, all of the instances I just listed are true examples of situations I dealt with in just one week of ministry.

Families all across the country are constantly faced with these dilemmas, and those same families are learning to rise to the challenge.

When do we force the rock bottom? How do we really help? It's terribly difficult to know, but to help an addict find their rock bottom, you can start by doing any of the things I just listed—and sticking to them.

And yes, I know that sometimes we do these things and nothing changes.

And yes, I know that sometimes we do these things and people still let us down.

And yes, I know that sometimes we do these things and people still die.

I know because all of those things also happened during that same week.

And it sucks. It hurt me. **I cried and got angry over it.**

But at least the parents tried everything they could to save their son. They forced rock bottom roughly a year ago and the son made it to treatment. He had a shot. He found some hope.

For whatever reason it didn't work. He didn't make it. **But instead of waiting on the elusive rock bottom they chose to act. They chose to step in and elevate rock bottom to give their son one last chance.**

If you're telling yourself you should wait to intervene until your loved one hits rock bottom, I urge you to stop. *You have a say in defining rock bottom.* So why not here? Why not now?

There's nowhere to go but up.

What Comes After Rock Bottom?

So, let's assume your loved one has hit rock bottom, and now you're wondering what to do next. Unfortunately, one of the main struggles I have in our family support groups that our ministry hosts, and even in writing this book, is getting the idea across that there *is no one-size-fits-all answer* to this question.

There is no clear-cut, step-by-step approach to handling your loved one's addiction. Anyone who tells you so, who guarantees "success", is lying to you or deceiving themselves. Each addict, although they have similar traits and motivations, is vastly different, just like your family is different from other families while still having some universal traits you all share.

While I can't offer you a line-by-line transcript of the

process you should follow, I *can* give you a template, based on my own personal experience and the education I've received. I can also offer you the hope that comes from seeing hundreds of addicts' lives changed as they've followed this template.

Before we go any further, let me encourage you with this: if your loved one has hit rock bottom and is wanting to make a change, *that's huge!* The road ahead is incredibly difficult, to be sure, but making it onto that road and being pointed in the direction of sobriety is a major victory.

Congratulations!

So let's talk generally about your options. My good friend Chuck Robinson, who works for Elements Behavioral Health as their National Director of Christian Programming and Outreach, likes to explain your options using the template of a baseball diamond. You know the goal in our American pastime: proceed around the bases until you make it all the way around, get home, and score a run.

Sobriety works in much the same way. I've identified four bases, and if the addict in your life can run those in order, they have a great chance of making it home. But what tends to trip people up, is thinking that a base hit is the same thing as a home run.

Look, hitting a ball through the gap between the second baseman and shortstop is a nice feeling, but don't think that double has brought them home. It hasn't. It just put them on base, and they have to go *all the way around* before it counts.

So, here we go.

First Base: Detox

Drugs and alcohol introduce a large level of foreign chemicals into the addict's physical system, and those chemicals have to be purged before anything else can happen. This is the time period called detox, and *it is the worst*. I'll never forget my 10 days in a detox facility, eating horrible food, living in green scrubs, having my vitals checked four times a day, and only seeing the light of day for the occasional smoke break. It was horrendous, and not just for me, the addict—it'll be hard for you, too. Seeing your loved one go through so much physical pain as the drugs leave their system, can be debilitating. *Both* of you just want it to stop. But, fortunately, it always eventually passes, and then they've done the first difficult part of scoring in baseball: getting on base.

Second Base: Residential Treatment

Once they've rid their body of all the toxins that their drugs or booze have put into them, your addicted loved one can head over to second base: residential treatment.

This is a period of time where the addict lives at a treatment center and their entire existence is overseen by a staff of professionals. Here, your loved one will learn an entirely new language, and be given new terminology to help them learn about themselves, about their disease, and what a way forward looks like.

I cannot state this loudly enough: *learn that language.* This is another thing Chuck Robinson taught me, and it's is so crucial because that new language is going to be their new lifeline, the thing that keeps them on track, and the mandate by which they live their new, sober life. By learning that language as well—by digging into the incredibly dense new vocabulary they'll have—you'll be able to encourage, support and *understand* them.

They will also begin to learn to love themselves.

So many people turn to addiction because they don't love themselves, and turning off the addiction isn't going to change that. Residential treatment provides a means for them to start the lifelong process of accepting who they are, and learning to love that person they see in the mirror.

Choosing the right treatment center is a tough process as well. Treatment is not a one size fits all type of scenario. Different facilities have special focuses, disciplines and therapies of choice. Some work well with mental health components, while others focus primarily on the drug and alcohol abuse. Some use experiential therapy while others use traditional approaches. Some have strict guidelines; others provide a looser environment. Treatment facilities are just like any other business; they will do some things really well and others not so well. So understanding what facility best suits you're loved-one is a road you need to walk down with someone else. It's a crucial step in the process and a choice that shouldn't be made flippantly.

Our organization, *Hope is Alive Ministries* would love to help you down this road. We work with hundreds of families every year helping them understand the best options for their loved one. We would be glad to visit with you, discuss your situation and present you the best options for your loved-one.

Third Base: Sober Living

This is a base that a lot of people try to skip, but my experience has taught me that sober living is critical for lifelong sobriety. Once your loved one leaves residential treatment, it is often impossible for them to reintegrate into normal society. Unfortunately, they do not tend to have all of the tools necessary to manage the transition, and a huge statistical majority of them will wind up back in rehab at some point in the near future if they try and skip this base.

What can you do to mitigate that recidivism? Sober living. Don't tell the addict in your life this, because it will freak them out, but if they'll commit to spending a year in a sober living home, they're *far more likely* to achieve lifelong sobriety. In fact, my recent experience tells me that eighteen months is really the best scenario.

Most of the addicts I encounter are young, so I always put it to them this way: they have probably 60 years left of their lives, give or take. I tell them that if they'll give one single year to sober living, they'll have a great chance at having the other 59 years be great ones. If they don't, they'll probably have a lot fewer years, and they'll be miserable for all of them.

Home Plate: Continued Meetings

After a year in a sober living home, most addicts are back on their feet. They've learned how to manage their lives, they've learned how to hold down a job, how to stay organized, how to maintain healthy relationships, and all the other stuff that normal living entails.

But they aren't done.

I recommend that they still attend regular meetings. This is the overlooked aspect of maintaining sobriety, but it's an imperative part of it. I've been sober for years now, and I still go to (and run) meetings all the time. I need to be reminded of who I was, so that I never lose sight of who I am now, and who I want to be in the future.

And one more thing: there's nothing that says *you* can't get involved in recovery, too. In fact, I recommend it! If you're successful in getting your loved one to get help, it would do you well to get help yourself. Get involved in Al-Anon or some other organization for family members of addicts. Learn the language. Let it change you. Give back.

Your health is at stake here, too. Take care of yourself.

Parent's Perspective: Wendell Lang

I knew so little about addiction when we got involved with Lance's recovery process. God graced our family by providentially getting us in touch with people who directed us to Rob's Ranch, a recovery facility that God used in a mighty way. The detox process is horrible for both the family and the client, but the necessary pain is essential for healing. Recovery is paramount to a computer refreshing, the old need to go away to get a clean screen.

Detox is necessary to rid the body of impurities and toxins, because these poisons must be removed before recovery is possible. The Bible uses a word for the detoxing process: purity. The meaning is to be utterly sincere, honestly transparent. Purity means to be clean. The word Jesus used was *katharizo*, from which we get our word "catharsis." Jesus said, "Blessed are the pure..." A better meaning of purity means to be unmixed or undiluted. Pure gold doesn't have any mixture of other metals. This spirit of undivided loyalty will allow our body to operate as intended.

Lance going to treatment was a time of anxiety, fear, and yes, hope. Hope has become the mantra for our family, and the first shred of hope began to crystalize throughout the treatment process.

This chapter has me thinking about two words: "no shortcuts." Lance made an attempt at a "short cut" approach to recovery and it simply did not work. While God can use any method in the healing recovery process, I am convinced that long-term accountability is the most effective and will yield the highest results of recovery.

Throughout my years of pastoring, I had always been the one doing the counseling and had never participated in personal counseling. The times of meeting with our counselor were unbelievably revealing and helpful to bridge a huge chasm in our family. It became apparent to me that not everyone views an event or circumstances through the same lenses. Each person brings a unique experience to a conversation.

For us we found that talk, time, and a lot of tears brought about healing and hope.

Treatment comes in many forms today, but I am convinced that a holistic approach to treatment is essential. A good treatment center deals with the *head*. This enables the client to think the right thoughts.

A good treatment center also deals with the *hands*. This allows the client to work in a constructive manner in service to others.

And finally, a good treatment center deals with the *heart*. This allows the client view his or her situations from God's perspective.

No one treatment center is right for everyone, so ask and research. Finances and faith in the institution are vital in choosing a treatment center.

8

THE MOTHER'S PRAYER

When I look back over my story, having more and more angles from other people to help me reconstruct that story more fully, I'm always amazed at the weight my mother carried. She is an incredible woman who suffered in silence at the hands of her smooth-talking, unscrupulous son, but who never gave up on him.

I've noticed this a lot as I've talked over the years with different addicts in various stages of recovery. Inevitably, when hearing about their relationships with their parents, I almost always hear something about the ways their mother had tried to help, and the strength she displayed in the face of the terrible havoc that addiction wreaks. Even when people don't have good relationships with their parents, the majority of the time, they still speak fondly of their mothers.

Moms, you have a terrific impact on your kids.

So, with this in mind, I want to turn this book over to my own mother for a moment. I asked her to write something about addiction from a parents' perspective, just like you've been reading, and she sent me 2000 incredible words that are unsparing in their assessment of where I used to be, while also full of grace and compassion. Want to know what's going on in the heart of the mother of an addict? Here you go...

It Got My Son

There is a tremendously thin tightrope parents struggle to walk. You work to be omniscient in order to protect them from evil that is lurking. You strive to see their vulnerabilities and train them to overcome... to be strong when temptation raises its ugly head. This is what I desperately wanted to do for my children. I had seen the absolutely devastating effects of drug abuse and alcoholism in my husband's family—how it took lives, how it destroyed relationships, how it left family members poverty-stricken.

My husband had nursed his father (with whom he had never lived) as he lay dying in a nursing home with an acid-eroded esophagus from decades of alcohol abuse. We had seen so many divorces it was hard to remember in-laws' names. We experienced family members going from owning businesses and living in nice homes to begging us for money.

It was ugly, and I wanted my children to see alcoholism and drug abuse for what it truly was.

As a parent, I tried to live out the principles of scripture as laid out in Deuteronomy 6 where it says, "These commandments that I give you today are to be on your hearts. Impress them on your children. Talk about them when you sit at home and when you walk along the road, when you lie down and when you get. Tie them as symbols on your hands and bind them on your foreheads. Write them on your foreheads. Write them on the door frames of your house and on your gate."

When bad choices cost people or took people's lives… it was the lesson I taught. When people made good choices and God blessed them, I gloriously set their example as a trophy in front of my children. My husband made sure they were surrounded by godly, Christian men and women. We had missionaries, evangelists, pastors, and denominational leaders intentionally in our home for them to learn from and hopefully emulate. I talked to them about how important it was to never take that first drink or experiment with that first drug due to the rampancy of abuse in our family. At the breakfast table each morning I prayed with them and for them. I searched for age-appropriate devotional books for us to read together, we memorized scripture… I strove to fully arm them as they left my nest.

Yet, it got my son.

Did I see it coming? Lance was strong-willed, incredibly capable, always the leader, always out front, always first… always pushing the boundaries, so did I see it coming? I guess I worried he would get into some situations where he would try stuff and we would have to discipline and pull back the reins, but I *never* thought bad choices would totally alter the whole course of his life. I had been too proactive for that to happen... but yet it did.

In the course of a few months he went from being a high school graduate enrolled for college in the fall, to being a teenage husband and father. I find out a decade later that he had begun to dabble with weed his senior year of high school which led to a whole pattern of bad behavior.

Was I *blind*? How did I not catch this? How did this happen under my watch, under my roof... am I the worst parent in the world? Did I not do enough to prepare him for temptations, did I not pray enough, was I not strict enough or was I too strict, did I not check out his friends and activities closely enough? If I allow them, these questions continue today to eat me alive, to suck the very life right out of me. Why...

Because, it still got my son.

Since we became pros in the addiction/recovery world over the last few years, I have discovered a new word...the word is enabling. Evidently, many times alcohol or drug addiction is the result of one or both parents enabling their child not to grow up, to remain dependent, to not accept responsibility...in other words, to do too much for them. So I have self-examined. I have searched myself; I have pondered and I have scoured my soul. My conclusion: I guess I did.

What I thought was empowering maybe was enabling; what I thought was giving good gifts to my children maybe was spoiling; what was pushing them to popularity and success in a lot of activities maybe was imposing my life upon them. All

I do know is this: I wanted them to have the very best life possible and be thankful; I wanted them to be godly, holy Christians that made a difference in their world; I wanted them to respect authority and above all fear their God, for this truly is the beginning of wisdom. I tried my best, *I failed a lot*, I have regrets, I would do things differently today, but unfortunately we don't have mulligans in raising our children. My intentions were good...

Yet, it still got my son.

So what do you do?

I tried denial and found it to be awesome. I joke about having lived in six states, but the best of them all is the state of denial. For many of the years Lance struggled with addiction, we lived three states away. We would visit regularly, but really knew little about his day-to-day life, the pressure he lived under, the pace he kept. However...there were signs.

When his marriage began to fall apart, we blamed it on them being too young when they married.

When he began seeing his children less and less, we blamed it on it just being too painful.

When my brother, his boss, would complain to us about his work performance, we would blame it on an overzealous boss.

When my mother-in-law questioned us about missing pills after Lance would visit her out of the blue, we would blame it on her memory.

When our daughter called crying after childbirth because Lance was in their bathroom and now her pain medication was gone, I finally confronted him. He apologized, he said he was really struggling and just needed to sleep and I accepted his story... I loved denial.

I remember on one New Year's Eve, Lance was leaving our daughter's house to "go out." I was recovering from a fall that left me with a cracked skull and debilitating headaches. I had fallen a second time as a result of the headaches and fractured my shoulder and my husband's stepfather had just died. I was cognizant enough to realize this night, of all nights of the year, is a recipe for bad choices, so I tried guilt. I remember telling him I cannot physically take anymore, please do not do anything stupid, to which he responded, "I never do anything stupid, I always make good decisions." And I blindly, ignorantly bought it.

My husband and I both knew he was in a bad place. Why didn't we do something? That will haunt me forever. We were so spineless. We did not want to believe this was our son and this had happened to us.

I feel so much compassion and empathy for parents who, like us, are struggling with *adult* children making these choices.

What do you do? What *can* you do? We should have been more confrontational, we should have intervened, we should have stepped in and gotten him help... yet we remained in denial until that same overzealous boss, my brother, stepped in and said, "This stops today."

What we should have done, we left to someone else. I have apologized repeatedly to Lance for this, and will continue to for the rest of my life. We knew… we lived in denial. The Bible recounts the story of Deborah in Judges 4-5. When times were tough in Israel the Bible says, "Deborah, a mother in Israel arose." I should have been Deborah, I should have arisen and met the problem head on, yet I chose to live day after day in denial.

Would it have worked if I had risen to the occasion? Only God knows if the timing would have been right. I believe there are times when a parent can do too much and they have to let the addict hit "rock bottom." I believe God did that with Israel on numerous occasions until they decided to look to him in repentance.

I remember after my husband and I moved back to Oklahoma after five years in Tennessee where he was pastoring. There were many reasons Wendell and I decided to move back, but a large one was the downward spiral Lance was on, and the negative effect it was having on our grandchildren. We wanted to be close to the situation and Lance refused to let us.

I recall one painful phone call I made to him telling him that I had his kids at my house and asking him to come over. I told him it had been five weeks since any of us had seen him, to which he responded, "Will you just leave me alone? I'll call you when I'm ready." I remember telling my husband, "Okay, that's it. I'm leaving him alone."

But in all actuality, I didn't leave him alone, because that statement brought me to the most desperate prayer I've ever prayed. I have to admit, I was angry at God *a lot*! I screamed at Him as I recounted my resume to Him. "God, I have believed you when you said train up a child in the way he should go and when he is old he will not depart from it. God, I had him in church, I tried to live it out home, I did all the right things…" and on and on.

Why, God, did it get my son?

I had to come to the place like Job in Job 13:15. The righteous, blameless Job was suffering unjustly and had every right to be angry with God, yet *chose* to say, "Even though you slay me, I will trust in you." I had to come to the place where my faith took hold and I believed afresh what God's Word said in Genesis 50:20 that what the enemy meant for evil, God would and could use for good. I began to pray, "God, whatever it takes…take me if it will turn my son around. I am willing to die if it will get his attention. God glorify Yourself, God we will give You all the recognition, honor, and praise if You will turn our son back to you. God, please allow him another opportunity to serve You, to be a godly man, to be a godly parent, to proclaim Your message of redemption and restoration."

And Praise the Lord, God got our son!

Please don't think I'm being a Pollyanna. I know many people who have similar life stories that end drastically differently, that end tragically.

My heart breaks for you.

I know His thoughts are higher than our thoughts, and His purposes are higher than our purposes. I know we now live in part but one day we shall fully know (I Corinthians 13:9). I know He loves us and His peace is a peace that passes our having to understand (Philippians 4:7). And I know He can take our messes and make a message for His Kingdom's sake. I know He can restore the years the locust has eaten (Joel 2:25).

In our family, God is restoring the stolen years in our grandchildren's lives; God is restoring the stolen years in our children's relationship; God is restoring the stolen years in our relationship with Lance; and God is restoring the stolen years of a wasted testimony and He is doing it in such an enormous way. God *is* able to do exceedingly, abundantly above all that we could ever ask or think according to the power that works in us (Ephesians 3:20).

The Mother's Prayer

Whew! Can you believe that woman? Can you understand why I love my mom so much? I'm so grateful that God has brought us both through my mess, all the way to this place where we have a great relationship based on the healing God has brought to us. So much so, that she's writing parts of this book!

The thing is: the whole time I was using, I knew my mom was praying for me. Even though I was so inwardly focused I could barely see to the end of my own nose, I still managed to occasionally glimpse the pain and hurt I was causing my parents. I knew my mom was praying for me because I saw it in her eyes. I watched her crumble slowly with each pill I took, with each poor choice I made, with each occasion when I didn't show up to a family gathering, or let my phone ring rather than talk to her.

When I *did* answer the phone, she would plead with me. She would always try to talk sense into me or quote scripture to me, but it always fell on deaf ears. I was just not in a position to hear her cries.

But God was. She prayed for me steadily through all ten years of my ordeal, forming every possible thought and shaping every sentence she could think of. She combined all kinds of words in prayer, all on the same theme: God, please save my son.

Eventually, however, my mom took a different track in her prayers, and I think it's one to consider if you're in the same situation she was in, loving a person who simply cannot shake their addiction. Her prayer became simple, but the slant on it was different than anything she'd prayed before:

"God, please do whatever it takes to help Lance find a relationship with you."

And you know what? He did.

What I love about this prayer is that any mother can pray it. Or father, for that matter. Or any loved one or any person who cares about another person. Just switch out my name for theirs and you're on your way!

"God, please do whatever it takes to help _____ find a relationship with you."

It's a risky prayer, though, because you have to mean it. The second you start considering the implications of that prayer, you tend to want to take it back. It's the *whatever it takes* part. That thought can be pretty scary, but it's also very necessary. The addict who simply came to their senses one day and left behind their addiction is extremely rare (and possibly doesn't exist—I know I've never met one).

So, if you're looking at a loved one who is far from God and close to an addiction, I would like to encourage you to be brave enough to pray this prayer for them. Moms, it can be tough, I know, but God loves your child even more than you do. You have to dare to leave them in His hands.

Interview With Other Addicts: Austin

Would you like the world to know your name? If so what is it?

My name is Austin.

In what ways did your parents or spouse try and help you quit using?

At first, my family simply tried to assume my addiction wasn't as bad as it seemed. Classic denial. As time went on (and my disease-related consequences mounted), they begrudgingly turned to a twelve-step program for the families of alcoholics/addicts. This proved to be a family-altering decision for all of us. From this point on, they stopped enabling me.

How many times do you think you thought about quitting?

Dozens of times. Not kidding; I recognized that something was wrong with me as early as 14 years old! And I actually attempted to stop at that age. There would be brief spells of being dry (I wouldn't call it true sobriety), but I always returned to the darkness. And each time I did, I would chase it harder than I ever thought possible.

What kept you from quitting?

Fear, toxic friendships, not buying into a twelve-step program, not being able to fully admit my powerlessness nor the unmanageability of my life, and ultimately believing that God was out to get me. Looking back, I had zero chance of success with these factors without a major overhaul.

You obviously found a rock bottom at some point. What was the final straw?

I had a really bad relapse that was public and very dangerous. From there, I was ushered to rehab. I relapsed at that rehab, and subsequently at the proceeding halfway house too. After coming to the realization that I had lost all control of my drinking and drugging, I came to the stark conclusion that this world would be better off without me.

I thought long and hard about taking my life. However, I distinctly remember a calming feeling that everything was going to be okay—I just needed to stop trying to fight this colossal challenge alone.

Ultimately, I finally chose to seek help with a willing spirit and found sobriety through a twelve-step program. This August, I will have 12 years sober; God willing.

Do you know if a loved one prayed for you while you were out using?

No doubt my mom did. My mom believes in the power of prayer as much as anyone I've ever met. She still to this day will rally her "prayer warriors!"

Interview With Other Addicts: Jake H.

In what ways did your parents or spouse try and help you quit using?

My first arrest was at 16; my mom called the police on

my friends and me, when we were smoking marijuana in my mom's house. My mom changed my high school three times, and sent me to my father's house for summers. I saw therapists. I had my phone calls recorded (back when there were land line phones). My bedroom door was taken off the hinges. I was shown everything from tough love to the *laissez-faire* attitude. Nothing my family did worked, except when I was cut out of their life completely, and given a choice… stay away or get help (and by help, that meant treatment).

How many times do you think you thought about quitting?

I used drugs and alcohol for 13 years. It wasn't until about the last 5 years of using, that I thought about quitting. But even during those times, I only thought about quitting for a brief moment at a time.

What kept you from quitting?

I always told myself that if I was able to pay my bills and live a comfortable life, then there was not a reason to stop. If my life was not affected in a negative way by my drinking or drugging, then I did not see a problem. That line between negative and neutral/positive, was blurred more and more as the disease progressed. Things I told myself I would never do when I was early in my addiction, were now things I did every day without thinking twice.

You obviously found a rock bottom at some point. How did that happen?

My family did not want me to be a part of their lives until I received help. I had no relationship with my family. I lost my apartment, my job, my car, my money. My health was fading. I was getting close to losing my freedom. I lost my self-respect. I just wanted to die, but I couldn't muster the ability to pull that trigger.

Do you know if a loved one prayed for you while you were out using? How do you know?

Absolutely! My mom prayed for me all the time. I know, because she told me. She would always tell me she was praying for me, and for me to do something different, that I was insane for doing the same thing over and over again and expecting a different result (That was before I knew that it was an AA saying!). She would tell me to try something different, and for *me* to pray about it.

When I actually decided to take my mom's advice and pray, my life changed drastically. My prayer was answered, but not really in the way I thought it was going to be. I thought I would just wake up and everything would be fine. It wasn't, but in about 1 to 2 months, I lost it all and had no choice but to go to treatment.

Interview With Other Addicts: The Addicted Child of An Addict

In what ways did your parents or spouse try to help you quit using?

My parents tried to help me quit numerous times. My dad would try to get me to go to AA meetings with him when he first got sober five years [before I did], however I was unwilling. Furthermore, he tried to get me connected with people in recovery. I was in denial of the fact that I had a disease and refused to listen to my dad and those who tried to help me.

How many times do you think you thought about quitting?

I thought about quitting hundreds of times. I tried only drinking or switching from one substance to another to no avail. No matter how many times I tried getting clean on my own, it did not work.

What kept you from quitting?

My unwillingness to admit that I was powerless and to turn my will over to God kept me from quitting. I was stuck in self-will and insisted on doing things my way. No matter what I tried to do and how I tried to do it, my way simply did not work.

So what's the story of how you found your rock bottom?

One would think that getting arrested and charged with felony drug possession with intent to distribute would be my rock bottom or close to it. However, I continued drinking and using for the next couple of years.

When I hit my rock bottom I was broke and in a large amount of debt, the girl I was dating was no longer speaking to me, my family had lost all trust in me, and I felt I had lost all hope.

A longtime friend had told my sister about the severity of my using and my sister told my dad, so he, my sister, and my grandmother planned an intervention. It was very emotional. I was extremely angry at my dad and I was heartbroken to see my sister and grandmother crying as they told me how much they loved me and how they detested the person I had become. I was finally at rock bottom and willing to do whatever it took to get my life back. That day I was off to detox and then treatment.

Do you know if a loved one prayed for you while you were out using?

My mom constantly prayed for me. She was worried sick about me and did not know whether or not I would live to see the next day. She would often tell me that she was praying for me to find peace in my life. I do not think that I would be where I am today if it was not for my Mom's continual prayer.

9

WILL THEY EVER BE FULLY CURED?

One thing most addicts—and their loved ones—want to know is this: will I be like this the rest of my life?

I was having lunch with a friend one day, and my friend has never been an addict, ever. He's a casual drinker who has a beer every now and then, and he likes to order special craft beers when he goes out to eat. Now, out of respect for me and my past, he's never ordered a beer when we've dined together (though I could tell he wanted to!), but during this lunch, the conversation turned to my past.

"Did you drink a lot of beer?" he asked.

"Oh yeah," I said.

"Oh, I figured that was too mild for a hard user like you."

"No, I still loved beer, too," I said.

Then he got thoughtful for a moment. "Are you, like, ever going to get to a point in your sobriety where you can, like, enjoy a beer with your dinner?"

I just looked him in the eye and shook my head. Not proudly, but not ashamedly, either. Just wordlessly stating the fact.

"Man," he said, trailing off and considering what that would mean for someone like him.

"That's just part of the disease," I said. And then we probably started talking about movies, not because it got awkward but because that's something we both love to talk about.

My friend is a good guy who completely understands the nature of addiction, but even he temporarily forgot the old saying: "once an addict, always an addict."

And for those who want to hear that their addicted loved one will be cured, that can be a major blow to their spirit.

But it's true. Addiction is not like a broken bone or a snakebite; something you can recover from fully and go back about your business like nothing ever happened.

No, addiction is much more along the lines of diabetes or heart disease—it's an ailment that requires a complete—and permanent—lifestyle change. If you have diabetes, you know you have to pay attention to the amount of sugars you take in, and there are just some foods that are off the menu. Same thing with heart disease: if you've had a quadruple bypass, you know you've already tasted bacon for the last time. In both cases, you must be vigilant—day in and day out—in order to preserve your health.

The same goes for addiction and recovery. This is not a temporary process; recovery is a lifelong journey. Once addiction impacts you, you live with it forever. It becomes the limp in your walk, always present, never leaving. But the hope I have for the loved one in your life—and for you—is that you will live both on the right side of recovery as long as you're taking breath on this planet.

Break Out of the Shells

I don't know how the phrase "walking on eggshells" came about. I don't know what it means, exactly, or what historical thing it's referencing. What I do know is this: I hear it a lot, especially from moms and dads, spouses, siblings, and other friends and family members of addicts.

I will meet with an addict's loved ones during the early stages of recovery, and inevitably one of them will say, "I just feel like I have to walk on eggshells around them." What they mean—and what you've probably meant if you've said the same thing—is that you're worried. You are living with the constant fear that anything you say or do could be taken the wrong way, and then they'll be out the door and headed for relapse.

It makes sense. After all, they weren't the most emotionally stable, rational person while they were using! They've trained you not to believe in their behavior, and they've trained you really well.

So what can you do?

First of all, realize that their sobriety is *their responsibility*, not yours.

One of the things they're learning is to take ownership of their decisions, which is something they hadn't done in the past (and why they were so irrational and moody). It's new to them, so it's going to be a little jarring and, just like a toddler does more falling down than walking at first, it's going to take them awhile to get used to it.

That's okay! You still can be kind and caring without littering your life with eggshells.

The other thing you *definitely* need in your life is a positive support group around you. You need to connect with other people who either have gone or who are going through the same ordeal as you, and who can provide encouragement to you through this time. And an extra bonus feature: *you* get to support *them*, too! It's a win-win!

Just like addicts need other addicts to lean on and to say, "I understand; I've been there," you too need other family members, spouses, siblings, or parents to say the same thing. You won't believe the tremendous emotional and physical benefits you'll get from regular interactions with other family members like yourself. I cannot encourage you enough to find a program and stick with it (in fact, we'll talk more about this later). Don't let anything stop you from doing this. Not pride, or fear, or telling yourself you don't really need it. None of that.

You need a support group. Join one!

The Right Way?

Have you ever heard that old story about the newly married woman who would trim the ends off a roast before she put it in the oven? After several meals of this, her new husband, curious about the methodology and wanting to know more about this fascinating little quirk of his wife, asked her why she did it.

"I don't know," she said. "That's just what my mother always did."

Now curious herself, the wife called her mother to find out why *she* had always trimmed the ends off a roast before putting it in the oven. And, adding to the mystery, the mother said, "You know, I don't know. It's just what I always saw *my* mother do."

As you can imagine, the next call was to Grandma, and the mystery was solved.

"Oh," said Grandma, "our oven was so small, trimming the ends off a roast was the only way I could fit it inside!"

Sometimes we think things are being done "the right

way" just because that's all we know. It's very easy to say, "Well, I did *this* and it worked for me, therefore it will work for everyone." And that may be true with some things, but I can tell you for a fact:

Addiction doesn't work that way.

There is no *one* way to find and maintain sobriety. Take it from someone who has visited dozens of facilities, spoken with counselors from all over the country, and lived with men representing ten different treatment centers: for every treatment facility that does things one way, there are ten others that do things ten *other* ways.

God made each of us to be unique individuals, and so there are lots of different ways to get the sobriety we all desire.

That said, I do believe that while sobriety can be achieved and maintained in a lot of different and specific ways, I also believe that millions of people have maintained sobriety using *generally* the same method. It's the method espoused by Alcoholics Anonymous.

In case you don't know the story behind AA and how it came to be, it's pretty incredible and something you should definitely read up on. There have been multiple books written about the program, about its founders, and about the spiritual underpinnings the entire process has, and I would encourage you to look them up and read about it; I think you'll find hope just within the story of AA itself!

I've seen the general method of AA get put to use in the

lives of many, many different addicts, and I've seen it bear fruit almost every time (I say "almost" because there are inevitably addicts who aren't quite ready to let go of their addiction just yet and who give up before they work through their entire program). Basically, there are five suggestions to help an addict get started toward living a healthy life alongside their disease. So I *suggest* that when your loved one comes out of treatment or is in early sobriety that you make sure they are following these suggestions!

1) 90 in 90

The first suggestion is to take the first 90 days *very* seriously. The way the addict shows they're doing this is by attending 90 meetings within those first 90 days.

Yes, that's really what I said. I cannot tell you how powerful this is—it was powerful when I did it, and it remains powerful when I see other people do it. This is a great first step toward getting your mind right and getting your body used to the discipline and organized structure of getting to the meeting, participating, and getting back home.

2) Put a Plug in the Jug

This one is kind of a no-brainer, but this is just a catchy way to say that it's time to stop using. Drugs and alcohol are no longer on the menu for the addict, and that starts right now. If you are a casual drinker like the friend I mentioned at the beginning of this chapter, you might consider showing support to your loved one by putting a plug in your own jug. Solidarity is a great motivator.

3) Find a Sponsor

I cannot tell you how invaluable my sponsor has been to me, especially in the early goings when I was bursting out of my mental seams with the desire to go do something stupid. Sponsors (we call them "hope partners" around here) are people who have been where the addict has been, and who have since found their way to long-term sobriety. They are a fount of wisdom, yes, but more than that, they're a willing, listening ear who will *always* be there for the addict, no matter what time of day.

You may be wondering whether you, as a loved one of the addict, can be a sponsor. My recommendation is that you do *not* try that. It seldom works and can tend to strain the relationship. Instead, just be a champion for them.

4) Work the Steps

This is another one of those things that sounds really obvious but can actually trip people up. There are twelve steps to recovery; you just have to work through them. I know that sounds simple—and it is—but you'd be surprised just how *hard* working through those steps can be. Have grace on your loved one as they go through this emotionally draining process, but encourage them to stick with it.

Some programs like Celebrate Recovery have "step studies" that are open to anyone; you may consider going through one of these yourself. You'd be surprised what you might learn about yourself; you may even find some ways the steps can help you get healthy in your own life!

5) Read the First 164 Pages of the Big Book

AA has a Big Book. It's really just that: a huge, big book, written by the AA founder Bill W., detailing all twelve steps, plus a whole lot of other stuff. It's a great resource, and is in a lot of ways a historically shaping text that changed our nation and the ways we think about alcoholism. The first 164 pages cover the basic groundwork of recovery and are, personally, very inspiring to me.

What About Relapse

If I'm telling you the honest truth in this book, then I have to be honest here: relapse is a part of many people's stories.

I would love to tell you that once your loved one finds sobriety that they will never, ever struggle again, but that wouldn't be the truth. Don't get me wrong, though: it's entirely possible that they will! That's what we always pray for, but statistically, they have, at best, a 50/50 chance of maintaining their recovery.

However, there are a few ways you can help game those chances in their favor: A sober living home (like what we run through Hope Is Alive) can have a huge impact; ongoing counseling beyond the residential treatment center is practically a must; and continuing to attend meetings is a perfect way to stay sharp.

But I'll say this: the most important part of my own sobriety has been keeping up a strong connection to my faith. My story has a lot of twists and turns, but Jesus, in the end, is the only reason I've been able to stay sober from day one. If I ever lose my total dependence on Him, I'm toast.

When Relapse Really Begins

Recently I heard someone say, "Everyone will relapse, but no one ever has to take another drink or do another drug." The more I pondered this, the more it made real good sense, but not only for the "addicted" out there, but for the general population as well.

I know *relapse* can be a dreaded word, and it carries with it a lot of negative connotations, so let's settle on a definition before we move any further. I believe *relapse* is defined as: "When, after a period of abstinence, a person re-engages in an activity that is painful to themselves or to others."

Relapse, backsliding, setbacks, regression, falling off the wagon… it doesn't matter what you call it or specifically what you are speaking to. The point is, *none of us is perfect* and we all have *moments* of relapse in our thinking, speaking, or even in our actions. The important thing to focus on is how you got about recognizing what you are doing and correcting your behavior so as to hopefully stop yourself from ever "taking that drink", "binging", "visiting that website" or doing whatever it is you're trying not to do.

Contrary to popular opinion, relapse does not start when a person decides to start using again. It's a long process of slowly migrating back into old behaviors, practices, or attitudes. Relapse really begins…

The moment they start to avoid accountability.

The times they skip out on your meetings because you're "tired."

The days they flip the channel to the free preview of the HBO show they know they shouldn't watch.

The nights they ignore their sponsor's phone calls.

The weekends they bail on the service work they used to be so committed to.

The moments they slip into negative thinking.

The stretches of time between their step work.

The days they fail to hit their knees in prayer.

The instants where they bury their secrets so they never see the light of day.

Relapse is a dynamic period of time. Its beginnings are eerily camouflaged, and its conclusions are oftentimes, public tragedies. Relapse can sneak up on people in their weakest moments, and lure them into poor patterns which lead to poor choices, which leads to pours, lines, clicks, and more.

But it doesn't have to be this way. The more addicts know about themselves, the better chance they have of catching themselves in the act of relapse behavior *before* they fall into the act of relapse itself.

Below are the four most common areas of *relapse*. These are elements of our lives that help us addicts quickly gauge how we are living, and how actively we are pursuing our choice to be abstinent. Like a barometer, the addict can measure themselves in these categories; but it doesn't mean a thing unless they're honest.

Run through these list of potential relapse questions and pay attention to your responses.

Area 1: Relationships

Check your relationship with God. Are you purposefully seeking a relationship with God every day? Are you harboring resentments against God? Do you find yourself angry at God?

How much do you love yourself today? This will always be evident in your self-care. Are you resting? Are you exercising? Are you taking time for you? Are you forgiving yourself when you make mistakes?

When we are using and abusing drugs and other substances, on average, we hurt 21 other people. Are you hurting others again? Are you mindful when you hurt someone else? Are you making amends?

Area 2: Honesty

Are you being completely honest with God, yourself and others?

Have you failed to tell the full truth recently?

Is there someone you need to be honest with?

Do you have secrets?

Area 3: Delusions & Denial

Are you beginning to negotiate with yourself in order to do things you haven't been doing or know you shouldn't?

Are you criticizing others?

Are you thinking poorly about others? Being judgmental?

Area 4: Letting up on Daily Disciplines

Are you justifying missing meetings, daily readings, church or family events?

Are you procrastinating on step work or calling your sponsor?

Are you avoiding accountability?

As the addict in your life read through these bullet points, if they nodded "Yes" more often than "No," then watch out: they're in the Kenny Loggins *Danger Zone*.

That doesn't mean it's the end of the world and the definitive close to your loved one's sobriety, but they definitely need to check their program, check their behavior, and talk to someone who cares about them (you, perhaps!). We are *all* just two choices away from relapsing, but staying true to ourselves and honest with others keeps us in where we need to be.

In the end, relapse is not some huge choice we make to drink, drug, or watch porn. It's the hundred small daily choices to do the wrong things over a period time, which leads to that one huge choice. But the great news is that relapse can be avoided the same way that sobriety can be found: by making the daily choice to do the next right thing in every situation.

Three Signs Relapse Is On Its Way

When it comes to relapse, there's a huge difference between someone who is early in their sobriety and those who have a few weeks, months, or years under their belt. No one is immune to relapse—"one day at a time," and all that—but just like a newborn baby stands a greater chance of catching a cold than a healthy teenager does, those who are new to sobriety *do* run a more significant risk of relapsing.

When you're learning to live sober, each day is a grind, and presents huge obstacles to overcome in order to stay clean. **The smallest of disagreements, comments, or change in the weather can send someone spinning directly back to their old ways.**

So you may be wondering: is there any way you can spot a potential for relapse *before* it actually hits? As it so happens, yes! As I've worked with different addicts over the years, I've come to notice three major signs that a person in early sobriety is headed down the road to a destination they want to avoid.

They Start Thinking They're Really Special

Let me say this: everyone is special in God's eyes. You are. Your addicted loved one is. I really hope you hear me on this so that no one gets me wrong or gets their feelings hurt. We are all beautiful, unique creations, purposefully created to do what only each of us can do.

But when it comes to the addict's recovery, they need to hear me loud and clear: "YOU ARE NOT SPECIAL!"

Those who are early into sobriety simply cannot go out and do their own thing and expect it to work. **There is a rea-**

son why they ended up where they did: because their way didn't work! They need to get used to doing things the new way; a way that countless others have discovered.

See, there is a solution to the problems that those who are recovering from addiction encounter, and that solution has worked for millions and millions of other people. It leads to a life filled with purpose, passion, and joy! It's a great life, but no one will get there by thinking they are immune to the rules, or that they can find their own way there.

Addicts: you cannot drag your old life into this new one; it has to stay behind where you left it so you can follow what has worked for others.

They Get In A Relationship

You know what the number one cause for relapse is? Romantic relationships. It's the biggest issue among people early in recovery. Why? Because newly sober addicts are not emotionally stable enough to handle the rigors of relationships.

Good, healthy, long-lasting relationships take a lot of work, and for the early seasons of your sobriety your focus needs to be on you, not anyone else. **That is why I fully subscribe to this tried and true recovery suggestion**: *No romantic relationships with anyone for the first full year of your sobriety.*

Now, most of the people I work with don't like this

rule, but here's what I've come to find out. The men and women who really want to stay clean will do what's proven to work for other people, while the people who really don't want it will think they're special (see the previous sign, in case you've forgotten about it during the last few paragraphs) and go jump in a relationship.

Look, relationships are emotionally demanding and require a ton of hard work—and that's when you're sober! Addicts shouldn't complicate their early sobriety by trying to cruise for their future spouse at an AA meeting. It just won't work and is an extremely bad idea.

They Refuse To Tell Anyone They're Sober

This is almost a guarantee for relapse: make sure no one knows they're trying to stay sober.

Now, it's not up to you to prod your loved one into telling their story of addiction and sobriety, or who they should tell that story to, but it's a great idea to be aware of how forward they are being with their struggle. If they're hiding it from everyone, not telling anyone at work or at church or at small group, then they're pointing in the wrong direction.

I know that can sound a little harsh, but it just wears me out to watch people struggle with relapse time and time again only to find out no one even knew they were trying to stay clean in the first place! **I tell guys and gals all the time:** you don't have to tell the whole world you're clean like I did, but the more people an addict can tell about the new life they're reclaiming for themselves, the more accountability they'll have when it gets rough.

If no one knows, no one can help.

Historically, sobriety has been an anonymous journey. And trust me, I understand why it started that way. **But in today's society, I think that can be counterproductive and only ends up limiting the social protection for an addict— and for the family of an addict**. Because you are not immune to the trials and tribulations of recovery, either. This is going to take a toll on you and all the other people who are in the same familial orbit as your loved one.

So just know: in the end, the more people who know what you're going through, the more people can help you when you have to go through a rough patch.

Why Is It So Hard to Stay Sober?

This is a question that a lot of addicts ask themselves, and it's probably something you as a loved one of an addict have wondered about as well. After all, the only thing sobriety entails is just *not* doing something, right? How can that be so hard?

To help you understand, I began asking this very question to some of the men I live with at Hope is Alive. These are all guys who have varying levels of sobriety, so to keep things straight and to add more poignancy to their answers, I've left their names out but have added, in parentheses at the ends of their responses, their length of sobriety at the time I asked the question. You ready? Let's hear from some recovering addicts on why it's so hard to stay sober.

"The hardest part for me is re-entering my own life. Learning how to actually deal with things like feelings and issues as they come up, and not trying to escape them. This is hard, but it feels really awesome to be truthful, and that prevents me from wanting to run from issues I typically run from." *(2 weeks)*

"The hardest thing about living a sober life is just that: 'sober life.' Just because I've gotten sober doesn't mean that life stops being tough. Life is life. There are good times and there are bad times, times of joy and times of pain. Life hasn't changed. What has changed is the fact that I no longer use drugs and alcohol as my solution. I was told when I got sober that if I stuck with it, my life would change. That hasn't been the case for me. What happened is, by working the steps and growing closer to God, *I've changed.* So life still happens, but with the steps, and most importantly, God, I am able to deal with whatever life throws at me." *(2 ½ years)*

"For me there are two 'toughest parts' about staying sober. One would be the 'legality' and availability of my drug of choice: opiates. I can have a legitimate prescription in my hands within an hour of having the itch, and I can justify it. I don't need a drug dealer—I have doctors, and they're much safer and cheaper.

Second, and most difficult, is dealing with emotion. For years I hadn't had to deal with emotions of any kind, because I could kill them with drugs. Since gaining my sobriety, I've had several crazy, emotionally draining, painful, exciting, relieving, and exhausting experiences. Literally, years' worth of experiences and emotions in a matter of a few months. When it got really tough, I knew there was an instant—albeit temporary—fix: swallow a handful of pills and feel no more. That's easy. But I've learned that turning these things over to God brings on a high so much more powerful, meaningful, rewarding, and gratifying than any pill has ever been. Watching God take the destruction of my past and the mistakes of my present and make miracles and testimony out of them has been amazing." *(5 months)*

"The hardest part of staying sober is, honestly, complacency. Back in my using days, most every day was a different 'adventure' of sorts. Different places to steal things from. Going out drinking and not really knowing where you might end up. Going out partying until 4:00 in the morning. But being sober, I don't get to do things like that. Most of my days are just about the same. It's taken some getting used to, but it's definitely a better way to live. Most things are predictable. Not many surprises are thrown at you in sobriety. Yeah, the occasional family emergency, sickness, death, or whatever will eventually come, but that's life. You learn to deal with these things like a normal human being instead of like a child. 'My dad died so I'm going to hole up in my room for 30 days straight and jab a needle full of drugs in me because that's what will make me feel better.' I know that doesn't work anymore, no matter how difficult life may get. What works is talking about these things. Feeling the feelings, acknowledging them, and getting on with my life." *(3 years)*

"I think the hardest thing for me at this point in my sobriety, is learning to go easy on myself. I have this golden standard that was set long ago by my family and it resonates still today. I can easily slip into a self-hatred mode if I don't reach perfection. But our literature talks of progress and not perfection. It's difficult to give myself a permission slip to not be the best _____ today. If I work my hardest at doing something, that's good enough for today." *(18 months)*

"The hardest part for me is having a mind that tells me it will be different this time. Because when I do think about using or drinking, my thoughts automatically go back to the good times. I don't go back to the time when I drank and drove and killed a man, or the times I was locked in a room by myself shooting coke.

Also, it's still hard for me to watch shows like *Intervention* or [media] that shows people shooting up. I can't watch anything with a needle, including having my own blood drawn. I think that's God's little way of telling me never to put a needle in my arm again!" *(2 years)*

"I don't get to do things like have sex with random women. I know that sounds crass, but it's true. Today the hardest part of living a sober life is living a changed life. My past life was comfortable, easy, and I knew how to survive. This new life is tough and challenging, but it's ultimately a whole lot more rewarding!" *(9 months)*

"The hardest part of being sober is staying consistent in my daily activities and responsibilities. Since becoming sober, I've picked up a variety of new responsibilities, including making time to go see my family, which has been difficult because they live in another town, maintaining my physical fitness, being on time, and doing what I am supposed to at work, leading others to try to stay sober, and continuing to grow my faith in God. Back in my using days I was just in charge of getting high for the day. That's all I focused on and all I cared about. But today, thank God, things are different and present new challenges." *(2 ½ years)*

"The hardest part about staying sober for me is staying in 'today,' staying present, and not playing too much in the future. Since I have such uncertainty about my future, my mind is constantly focused on preparing to go to prison, so I struggle to find peace. I also have a hard time dealing with trauma [because I] can no longer medicate it away." *(7 months)*

"Keeping a balance in life. The less life is about drugs/focusing on your initial sobriety and more about being a productive member of society, the tougher it gets to keep a balance." *(2 ½ years)*

"My life since getting sober is so unimaginably good that the hardest thing for me these days is remembering how awful life was, and would be if I went back to behaving like I use to. There have been times I've attended events that historically I would have drank or used at, and the struggle is convincing myself that, while the event might be more fun if I weren't sober, my life after that would change both rapidly and dramatically for the worse." *(3 years)*

Parents Perspective: Wendell Lang

The preceding chapter has dealt with the possibly of relapse. The reality of relapse must be dealt with in an "eyes wide open" approach. The old saying is true, "people don't do what you expect but what you inspect." We believe in the principle and spirit of hope, but what can you do to help your love one if there are no guarantees?

Pray. The psalmist said, "Pray for the peace of Jerusalem" (Psalm 122:6).

Be Gracious. "Let the peace of God rule in your hearts" (Colossians 3:15).

Believe the truth. Jesus said, "He who does not follow me, cannot be my disciple."

If you have a loved one who has lost their way, consider the following: In 1935 Bill Wilson and Dr. Bob Smith, from Akron, Ohio, developed a twelve-step process of recovery for people addicted to alcohol. This was the beginning of Alcoholics Anonymous (AA) and these same twelve steps based on scripture have been adopted and adapted by numerous other recovery groups. They work eventually, if your loved one can't work them originally. Countless people have been helped and stayed sober and clean. There is hope for you!

10

FINDING HOPE

This book all started because of a class. It was a class called "Finding Hope" (great title, right?), and I started hosting it for family members of addicts so they could know what to expect and learn how to move forward with an addict in the family, whether that addict was in active recovery or not.

It was, as you can imagine, quite the roller coaster for everyone who came. I had so many things I wanted to teach them, so many chains I wanted to break, and so many assumptions I wanted to overturn, and that started with empathy.

We've covered some of this ground already, but too many people automatically assume that an addict is some grungy, good-for-nothing, spineless coward who grew up in a home full of child-hating atheists. And while this *can* be true, it isn't remotely accurate across the board.

The truth is, addicts can come from anywhere. I know

a lot of addicts who came from great homes, with parents who loved them and provided well for them, who grew up in church and who can quote the Bible with the best of them. Most addicts I work with are good-hearted people who have been waylaid by their addiction. They're broken and wounded, but they aren't *evil*.

To demonstrate this to those who came to our Finding Hope class, I brought in some of the men who are involved with Hope Is Alive, men who are on well on their way to recovery, who have captured sobriety and who are holding on to it for dear life. These men are nice, respectful, clean-cut, honest guys, and I would trust (almost!) all of them with my life.

But this was one of the things that wound up having a great impact on those who came through the class. I think we tend to have a slight, intimidating fear of those who are not like us. We unconsciously divide our world up into "people who are like me" and "people who are not like me," and we feel comfortable around that first group and extremely uncomfortable around that second group.

We tend to want to slot addicts into that second group, but one thing the folks in my class began to learn as they interacted with the men from Hope Is Alive, was that most addicts are really largely in that first group.

They're just people. Just like you.

Broken, like you.

Hurting, like you.

In need of forgiveness, like you.

Called to love, like you.

Loved by Jesus, like you.

Anyway, near the end of our first session of classes, we went around the room and recapped what everyone learned and what were the best takeaways. Here are a few quotes from the parents, spouses, and other loved ones who attended.

"I wish we had this class and learned all of this years ago."

"The boys and all they had to say—I learned so much from them."

"Tough love and setting boundaries are really important."

"Letting go is necessary."

"Loved knowing about the 'new language' you need to learn to speak; I feel like pounds have been lifted off my shoulders."

"I'm more relaxed now. I can pray with more confidence after hearing all the boys say that God is what has gotten them through this."

"I can let go of pride; I have to fix myself, too."

"I don't have to carry this load anymore. I can finally say there is hope"

Then we asked which part of the class was the most difficult thing for them to hear and take in.

"Loved one having to hit bottom."

"Bringing up all the old stuff that I had hidden inside of myself."

"The word 'relapse.'"

"The word 'treatment' repeatedly."

"Stories about parents getting phone calls in the middle of the night and becoming fearful of getting a phone call that my child is dead."

"There is no 1-5 step you can put your addict on to fix them."

"Death."

"Hearing these young men talk about the choices that they made and then hearing the anguish over those choices"

"Discovering that I'm being an enabler."

"Finding the boundary of line of co-dependency and love."

"Learning that I can't fix them."

"When I pray and pray and God doesn't fix the situation."

These are likely some thoughts you might be thinking or feelings you might be feeling as well. That's okay! It's tough to see a loved one or family member go through pain, and even tougher to acknowledge the roles you can and cannot play in helping them find themselves again.

But on top of all these thoughts and feelings, the one thing we heard over and over, the thing that trumped all the good stuff and shone a light of hope on all the hard stuff, was a three-word phrase that almost everyone spoke:

"I'm not alone."

I believe, to the depths of my heart, that the best medicine for families living with addiction, is that empowering, life-giving knowledge that *you are not alone*.

I'm going to say that again, because I want to make absolutely certain you can latch on to this truth and lodge it in the innermost part of your soul—that's how important it is:

You.

Are.

Not.

Alone.

In case you don't know already, this is the guiding principle of small groups. The Bible is our best teacher of the value of the community, and the New Testament church showed us how to share not only in our blessings, but in our struggles as well. And when we can become united in our pain, but still under the banner of love, we can begin to find hope.

We find hope when we can sit among others who have the same struggles and victories as we do, and vulnerably share about what we are facing in our lives. We exhale deeply, shaking internally as we speak of the terror, the fear, the embarrassment, the confusion, and the doubt we feel…and then weep with strength as we watch as dozens of heads nod in agreement and tears fall in unison.

Then and only then can we grasp this majestic feeling of HOPE. Together we are

Holding

On

Praying

Expectantly

So how do you find hope? You find help.

Help from God.

Help from others.

And yes, help through yourself.

This can be one of the most difficult lessons for a family member, or spouse, or parent of an addict, but it's a hard truth: it is more important for you to focus on *yourself* than it is on the addict you love. Their health and long-term potential of finding the life-giving gift of sobriety rests on their ability to get healthy, but it also rests just as much on *you getting healthy as well.*

If I've seen it once, I've seen it a hundred times. The addict goes to treatment, gets out and relapses. They fall further, cause more pain and then go back to treatment, get out and relapse again! This process is then repeated time after time after time. Except near the end something changes. The parents or spouse finally begin to understand the role they play in this diabolical drama, and they start getting help for themselves. They find a Celebrate Recovery meeting to attend, an Al-Anon group to be apart of, and as they begin to find health, miraculously, the addict begins to find a solid foundation of sobriety.

It's hard to believe, but trust me this is true. An addict's recovery is often time pursuant to the family finding recovery. Or better said, your addict finds HOPE, when you FIND HOPE!

So getting help for yourself must be a priority. In fact, I believe you should deem your health more important then the health of your addict.

I know that can seem counterintuitive, but it's just the plain truth. And it's okay to think that way! A lot of times people—especially people of faith—feel prideful or selfish when they prioritize their own physical, emotional, or spiritual health over others. But this is a fallacy! Jesus gave an explicit command to "love your neighbor as yourself," but within that command is an implicit assumption: that you love yourself. You can only love your neighbor, your child, your spouse, or your other family members as well as you love yourself. And that means you must take care of you.

11

GIVE IT AWAY!

There's an old song that I grew up with, and the chorus lyrics go like this: "Now that you've found love, what are you gonna do with it?" I think of this song often, but I switch it up. Instead of "love," I say "HOPE."

So now that you've found HOPE, what are you going to do with it?

Recovery will be a lifelong journey, both for you and your loved one. When addiction settles into the life of your loved one, it settles in for life. This truth is simple to say but difficult to accept, but that doesn't make it any less true. Your spouse, or son, or daughter, or parent, or family member will face this struggle for as long as they are alive.

It's my belief that the most successful families are those who embrace the plight of addiction and the rewards of recovery. I haven't come to this belief through a theoretical framework or a series of thought experiments—I believe this because I see it over and over.

Basically, when your child or spouse finds recovery, then you need to as well!

And a large part of recovery is the principle of giving back.

The Unfair Advantage of Your Story

It never ceases to amaze me how often people come up to me and tell me how inspired they are by me. Or how they love what I am doing and are challenged by it. I hear it all the time, and I assure you it has nothing to do with my speaking or writing ability, but everything to do with God and this unfair advantage he has given me through my story of hope.

You see, I have something that no one else does. And so do you. it's called *my story*. It's perfectly mine and specifically purposed to help others. But so is yours! Because, as unique as each of us are, our struggles are oftentimes universally experienced. What I've gone through, so have others. What you are experiencing, so are others.

You have a story to tell. Don't sit on it, and don't let it go to waste. No matter where your story is today, someone needs to hear it. You may have emerged with a third-act victory that would inspire even the darkest soul, or you may currently be mired in a terrifying, second-act cliffhanger, dangling by the strength of your fingertips, and wondering whether you'll be able to find firm footing again.

However far your story has progressed, you have what someone else needs to hear.

When you can begin to see your situation—no matter what it looks like—as a blessing, then you can use it to change the world.

Real people, who have gone through real issues of pain and suffering, have what Mike Foster, the founder of People of the Second Chance, calls "the Unfair Advantage". You have lived through a tragedy, stood on death's doorstep, and now you have an unfair advantage, because you have found something the whole world needs.

Hope.

Hope is what sets you free to live again. Yes, your situation with your loved one might just be beginning. But now you have the hope to know that no matter how dark it may get, God will never leave you stranded without help. Or maybe you're in the throes of it, stuck right smack dab in the middle of the hell that is addiction. Today you can smile knowing that the best choice you can make is the one that gives you the medicine you deserve. Or maybe you're in a recovery story, seeing the lights come back into your loved one's eyes. You can look back on the hope that sustained you through the darkness and know you'll be able to rely on it in the future, all while passing it on to others who were just like you.

We were created to give hope to the rest of the world. Our experiences give us the unfair advantage of HOPE.

Hope is the key ingredient that is missing in the lives of hurting people.

Finding hope helps soothe the hurt.

Your story, which is always being written, is a deadly tool that can be used to shut down the enemy's fiercest attacks. Our brothers and sisters desperately need to see you standing up boldly and sharing your story, however "crazy" it may be, so that they can see that hope does exist and it's still alive!

Interviews With Other Addicts: Jeff L.

How is your relationship with your parents now that you are sober?

My relationship with my parents really could not be better. Not only do they allow me to be around them, they really *want* me to be around them! They trust me completely, they respect the life that I live, and they have both told me multiple times how proud they are of me.

Since you've been sober, what are some of the things your loved ones have made you do to make you earn back trust?

The first thing they made me do is to not only go to

sober living, but be a leader and challenge myself in sober living. For the first 18 months of my sobriety, I had a reloadable debit card and I could never have more than $30 on it at a time. I was also unable to access cash from the ATM with this card. I wasn't able to have a car until I held down a job for 6 months.

What have you seen your loved ones do that has helped them the most throughout this process?

The main thing my parents did that helped them, was coming to the treatment center every single weekend to have a sit-down with my counselors and me. This gave us the opportunity to express ourselves without there being any major problems. The counselors could correct any errors in our thinking, and we could all find positive solutions to our issues. They also attended the family weekend that helped them realize how they enabled me in my addiction, and gave them tools to stop the cycle. My mother also attended Al-Anon while I was in treatment.

Do you think you would be clean today if your loved ones had not gotten the help they also needed?

I kind of think I would be. I'm a grown-up now and the decision was mine to make. That being said, the decision was a lot easier to make knowing the consequences that were pending had I messed up again. My parents being stern and drawing a clear line in the sand made it perfectly clear to me where I stood and what would happen if I didn't get my life straightened out.

What's it like to have a healthy relationship with your parents today?

It is honestly the best part about recovery. It was so stressful having to lie all the time, and my parents being the people that loved me the most in the world, they had to hear the vast majority of my lies. It is so nice to see a phone call from my mom and not cringe. It is so nice to see that phone call and gladly accept it because I love to talk to her and can't wait to hear what she has to say. I also love the fact that every single time I talk to my dad, he tells me what they are fixing for dinner and offers me an invite and is actually disappointed when I can't make it.

Interviews With Other Addicts: Michael G.

How is your relationship with your loved ones now that you are sober?

My relationship is the best it has ever been. I have not been sober as an adult, and to have an adult relationship with my parents is a true blessing. We have communication like never before. I actually value their opinions and don't feel like its always judgment come down on me. I don't feel the guilt I once had that made it difficult to obtain this relationship.

Did your loved ones (in this case your parents) set any guidelines or rules to help you earn their trust once more?

Time is my biggest ally in gaining their trust back. My parents did not set down guidelines... after they went to Al-Anon, they just took it day by day, like I do. Over time, I have proven that I am serious about my recovery, and this has built some trust back. I just need to keep doing the next right thing and it will work out.

What have you seen your parents do that has helped them the most throughout this process?

Seeking help for themselves.

Do you think you would be clean today if your parents would not have gotten the help they needed?

No because the guilt of the pain I have caused them would weigh heavy on me. It is easier to become healthy when the ones you love are becoming healthy as well.

What's it like to have a healthy relationship with your parents today?

Great. I can see the pride in their eyes, and I look for-

ward to spending time with them. I call them out of the blue
just to talk.

What was the best thing your parents ever did for you?

Not enable me anymore, but offer help to get into rehab.

Parents' Perspective: Pam Lang

James 1:17 says, "Every good and perfect gift is from
above and comes down from the Father of lights with whom
there is no variation or shadow of turning." How I bless my
gracious Heavenly Father for the gift of my precious son's re-
turn from the miry clay. How I bless my forgiving Heavenly
Father that He has given all of my family a second chance to
be a family. How I bless my protective Heavenly Father that
Lance is alive, not in prison, and that he did not physically hurt
anyone while under the influence. How I bless my restorative
Father that He has given my son the opportunity to make a
"message out of his mess." When I think of how drastically
different things could be, I can do nothing else but fall on my
knees and thank my God of the second chance.

Most people in my season of life look back at their
children's graduations, weddings, and the births of their grandchildren as some of the most wonderful days of their parenting.
Indeed I do. But I also add events such as Lance's transition

from rehab, when he first began telling his story of redemption and recovery, when he started making restitution for past poor choices, and when he dedicated his life to giving hope to men and women entrapped in addiction.

I remember two occasions I whispered in his ear, "Thank you for giving me one of the best nights of my life." The first occasion was at the book signing for his first book, *Hope is Alive*, and the second time was at his first Night of Hope event. I got to see what I knew was there all along: my extremely gifted, capable son using all of his talents and abilities for good. I got to witness him give instead of take; I got to see him share truth instead of lies; I got to see him share hope instead of living hopelessly.

2 Corinthians 1:3-4 says, "Praise be to the God and Father of our Lord Jesus Christ, the Father of compassion and the God of all comfort, who comforts us in all our troubles, so that we can comfort those in any trouble with the comfort we ourselves receive from God." That has become my mantra. I will not waste this suffering.

My husband and I desperately want to comfort parents who are in the throes of dealing with a child ensnared by addiction. Not that we have any great words of wisdom or counsel that will automatically restore their child, but we do know that our Father God has all the answers. What we can do is boldly approach the throne of grace on their behalf. What we can do is comfort them, love on them, encourage them, and walk through the nightmare with them.

How I wish I could transport my friends to the other side when I see them going through what we went through. But I can't, so instead I pray and check on them and try to get their child into a recovery program. We listen to them weep uncontrollably and wring their hands and blame themselves and use all their savings or retirement monies. It seems like you are in a black hole with no way out. So we do what we can to comfort them in their affliction in the same way God comforted us in our time of affliction.

May I repeat myself? *We will not waste our trial*, although it would be much easier to distance ourselves and allow pride to conquer. It would be incredibly simpler to allow shame to silence us, to allow guilt to rob us of any joy; but rather I proclaim to you that we will use our suffering as a platform to display our God of Hope, the only hope for any of us as we traverse our broken world.

One of my life verses in holy scripture is Psalm 40:1-3: "I waited patiently for The Lord and He inclined to me and heard my cry for help. He brought me up also out of a horrible pit, out of the miry clay and set my feet upon a rock, and established my goings. And He has put a new song in my mouth, even praise to our God, many will see it and fear and shall trust in The Lord."

I pray your child or loved one gets out of the horrible pit and miry clay of addiction. I pray that when they do, that your family will choose to comfort others in their affliction. May we all indeed sing a new song of praise and thanksgiving as God restores and brings hope to the hopeless, may we with our lives, mouths and testimonies indeed proclaim, "HOPE IS ALIVE."

Parents Perspective: Wendell Lang

We were given some signs that our kid had a problem, and I wish the first time someone had given me this hint, that I'd known what to do. That I'd been strong and I'd been decisive. Parents, you'll understand this, but sometimes when you don't know what to do, you'll just do nothing, and that can later on be interpreted as denial or enabling or blessing poor choices, but that wasn't what it was. For me, it was just standing there knowing our family had to move in one direction or the other, but not knowing which way to go.

But once we found out for sure that we had a major-league problem with Lance, there was no anger. Yes, there have been times of shame all through this, and even to this day, this scab can get knocked off and it's painful, but the main emotion I felt was determination. I was ready to do whatever it took to get healing for Lance and for the rest of us. That trumped all embarrassment and any kind of personal pain. And it started us down a road that we never dreamed we'd be on.

The most painful thing for us was to see Lance in detox. When those toxins were coming out of him, seeing him stand up and literally kick his legs to get that poison out of his system, there in the lowest, shabbiest place in Oklahoma City. That was hard. The pain of that as a parent… you just want him to get better. The philosophy of addiction didn't matter right then—I just felt a heaviness and a vicarious pain for Lance and for his mother.

But from that pain came good. Now Lance is giving back. He's in churches almost every Sunday telling his story; his books have helped countless people; and we are able to refer people to treatment through Hope Is Alive. I've never had an opportunity, and it seems weird, but I'm so happy. It's the sovereignty of God! I'll say time and time again, that Romans 8:28 doesn't say all things are good—it says that all things work *together* for good for those who are called according to the will of God.

Now we can see a clear picture of what God was doing with Lance. It's been providentially used to help a lot of people. There's a lot of hope in that and a lot of reasons to rejoice.

But there's some bittersweet part of it, too. My son gets up on Sunday mornings, gets behind the podium, and delivers a sermon… about how his life was wrecked by drugs. Of course I wish he was following my pastoral footsteps and was up there for a different reason. Of course I wish that he'd made great choices from early on, and that, together we all could have somehow circumvented some of the pain that he went through. Of course I do.

But I don't spend a lot of time reliving those moments of pain. Because I see people respond to the message of hope. I see people respond to dealing with excess in their own life, and of making poor choices. I see God using broken vessels.

We did everything right. I preached about spending time with family, and we did it. We took vacations. I was at the ball games. We had quality time. So Lance's addiction seemed unfair! It didn't seem legitimate, because we had "done it right." What happened?

I am one of Lance's biggest supporters now, and that's not just because he's my son. We parents want our children to succeed. That's why we play basketball in the driveway with them until it's dark; it's why we play catch in the backyard; it's why we go to soccer camp. When your child is involved in something, you do it.

My parents were a little more distant, so I was all in with Lance. I wasn't just going to the games—I wanted to go to the practice! That's part of my makeup, and part of why I support Lance's ministry now.

Another reason I support Hope Is Alive is simple: because it was, in a way, born on my porch. Lance had just been let go of a dream job, he was fairly newly sober, and we were sitting there wondering what was next. I asked him what was next, and though he remembers it a little differently than I do, that was where the ministry of Hope Is Alive was born. I got to be in on that!

But as a parent, I've grown happy to be in the John the Baptist role for HIA. I'm happy to decrease and let Lance increase. That's how I give back.

So now I ask you: you've been given a gift. How will you give back?

Closing by Lance:

So again, now that you've found HOPE, what are you going to do with it? The next steps are up to you. It's your turn. And that's really what recovery is all about. Stepping out with action to apply what you've learned, and to start making changes.

For you it may mean doing something you've never done, like cutting your child's finances off, changing the locks or leaving your son in jail.

Or maybe you are realizing that for years you've been traveling this road alone, and you are ready to find a support group that can begin to help you heal your wounds.

But I know for many, you may feel like you've just read the story of your child. But your son or daughter has yet to find sobriety. Well, today it may be time to call us at Hope is Alive and begin that journey of finding the right treatment facility.

Or maybe as you read the book, you began to realize your role in the problem and instead of your child getting professional help; it's time for you to get help. That's ok. We're all a little crazy remember? Call us at HIA and let us help you find the right counselor.

For you mothers, it might be that as you close this book. You hit your knees and pray the mother's prayer we discussed in Chapter 8. Fully giving your loved-one over to God, and accepting the outcome He provides.

Whatever you take away from this book, it's my hope that you will walk away realizing you are not alone, it's not your fault and there is hope!

Lastly, I pray this book challenged you to take action. To get in the game and not allow addiction to keep you strapped to the sidelines. Real change takes place when we choose to take real action. From action we find hope, and when we find hope, we discover a new life. A life of freedom, grace, acceptance and love. It's a beautiful life, a life you deserve.

Go find it.

ABOUT THE AUTHOR

Lance Lang has devoted his life to inspiring hope in all those he comes across. His powerful story of overcoming addiction has touched the lives of thousands of people across the country. Lance is a successful blogger and a sought after speaker who is known for his ability to speak directly to the heart of any audience. He is also the founder of Hope is Alive Ministries, a non-profit organization devoted to supporting men, women and their families recover from all types of addictions.

Connect with Lance:

    @LanceLang   Lance@LanceLang.com

HOPE IS ALIVE

This book is the story of how my hope departed, how it was restored, and how I've kept it alive. I wrote it for drug addicts, alcoholics, gamblers, sex addicts, hurt people, prideful people, and angry people. I wrote it for the fear-ridden, the guilty, the insecure, the obsessed, the perpetually disappointed, and anyone else caught in the tornado of destruction that is addiction.

THE HOPE HANDBOOK

The Hope Handbook is the corresponding guidebook that takes the reader deeper into each chapter, allowing them the opportunity to share about their personal experiences and participate in activities created to solidify the teaching while offering therapeutic times of mediation, music, and prayer.

HOPE CHANGES EVERYTHING

Dreams are universal. The hopes we all have for our future, the plans we all sketch out in our minds. And then, somewhere along the way, those dreams slip out of our grasp. Whether through some kind of pain or worry, some guilt or mistake, or just the dull routine of life getting in the way, we lose hope and start to slide into normality. But it doesn't have to be this way! Those dreams can fuel your world once more, you just have to discover the transformative power of hope.

hope**IS**alive
ministries

*Inspiring Hope * Building Foundations * Changing Lives*

At Hope is Alive Ministries we work hard every day to help people find hope. We work with families, addicts in addiction, addicts in recovery, pastors and church leaders, counseling professionals, interventionists and many more. Here are some of the ways HIA can help you!

HIA Mentoring Homes: We operate three Mentoring Homes for recovering addicts who are trying to turn their lives around. These are safe and structured places for men to start their lives over.

Finding Hope: Each week we offer support groups for parents and loved-ones of addicts along with separate classes for addicts in early sobriety. Find out more here: **www.FindingHope.Today**

Night of Hope: These engagingly creative and inspiring events provide help and HOPE to the community. We provide free education and resources to those actively affected by addiction.

Church Partnership Program: We consult and partner with churches to provide their staff a "first responder" in times of addiction crisis, while also providing their congregation with valuable resources and referral options.

Family Services: Hope is Alive provides referral services, interventions, family consulting and free resources to individuals all across the country. Visit **www.HopeisAlive.net/Resources** to find our list of trusted resources.

To find out more about Hope is Alive Ministries visit us at www.HopeisAlive.net.

Connect with HIA

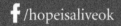 /hopeisaliveok 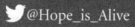 @Hope_is_Alive  @HopeisAliveOK

TRUSTED RESOURCES

OF HOPE IS ALIVE MINISTRIES LISTED IN THIS BOOK

Second Story Ranch

Sheila Ridley

www.secondstoryranch.com

405.679.0023

Transforming Life Counseling Center

Kyle McGraw

www.TLCCOK.com

405.246.LIFE

Elements Behavioral Health

Chuck Robinson

www.elementsbehavioralhealth.com

1.844.266.1919

Made in the USA
Middletown, DE
21 June 2019